HOOK

WHY WEBSITES FAIL TO MAKE MONEY

Andrew McDermott & Rachel McDermott

wisetoweb

Published in the United States of America by WiseToWeb

Hook and other WiseToWeb titles may be purchased in bulk for educational, business, fund-raising, or sales promotional use. For information please email contact@wisetoweb.com

ISBN-10:0990017206
ISBN-13:978-0-9900172-0-2

Table of Contents

Introduction

Creating a successful website is a challenge. For many businesses, making money with their website is a struggle. The average business owner is pulled in many different directions, experiencing failure after failure as they struggle to generate the kind of results they dream about.

Many business owners come to us with the belief that if they redesign their website things will be okay. If they create the perfect site things will begin to work and the money will begin to flow. It makes perfect sense why they fight tooth and nail to get things right.

Because in their mind, their success depends on it.

So they redesign their site. After it's launched they spend money on advertising. They move heaven and earth to get people to come to their site, they work incredibly hard to get the word out. Yet when they do, the results are still the same.

Customers refuse to buy.

It's a frustrating ordeal yet businesses continue to run on the treadmill, working tirelessly on small changes that fail to produce the results they want. Blown back and forth, they continue to chase after every fix that's presented. Every solution offered in hopes that one day it'll stick. That one day they'll find success.

This book aims to solve that problem.

Most business owners have been kept in the dark. If you're like them you've received bad advice: *Focus on the features and benefits. Customers don't read so keep your copy short. Avoid these colors, customers won't buy from you if you use them.* The kind of advice misses the point entirely.

Website failure is a business problem.

It seems so obvious to some, when they hear it they respond with "oh, I knew that already". But for many of us it isn't obvious, Which makes learning all the more painful.

What do we mean when we say it's a business problem?

Customers look for very specific things when they buy. In fact, the vast majority of us look for these specific things in most areas of our lives. And yet when it comes to websites, we receive training that tells us to give customers the exact opposite of what they expect. Pretty unfair isn't it?

And so our poor training teaches us to behave badly, to treat customers in a way that creates resistance. Which causes us to struggle, leading inevitably to website failure.

What you should expect from this book.

1. This book is about strategy. There are lots of great books on digital marketing. The problem for most business owners is that the majority of these books talk about tactics. How to use social media to generate traffic. Wordpress vs. Drupal vs. Joomla. SEO vs. PPC.

2. These tools aren't useful by themselves if you don't have a strategy or blueprint that dictates how to use them.

3. If you're looking for tactics, or information on how to use a specific tool or environment, this book isn't for you.

4. If you want specifics on the precise number of keywords you should add to your page or which social network buttons you should add to your site, this book isn't for you.

5. If you want clear direction on strategy (which then guides your tactics), This book was written just for you. Once we've explained the strategy, we'll show you how to use it.

Over the years we've learned from a lot of very smart people [1]. We've run hundreds of tests on behalf of our clients and we've gone through a significant amount of training. We've learned from other experts and we've used their training with our clients. A large part of our experience has been trial by fire. We've been in the trenches as business owners since 2005. We've experienced failure and success, and we know what it's like to struggle.

Who is this book for?

This book is for the frustrated business owner. If customers aren't buying from your website as much as you'd like them to, this book is for you. If your website (and business) struggles to compete with other websites and businesses, this book is for you. If your website isn't performing the way you'd like it to and you're unsure or unclear about why, this is for you.

How to use this book

This book is designed to be modular. It comes in two parts, Story and Method.

The story is just that--a story. It takes you through each of the concepts that we share in the method section. The examples, the problems and the consequences are all there. It's an amalgamation of fiction, our own experiences and stories we've heard from others.

The method section dives deep into the concepts conveyed in the story. You'll learn about how customers buy, what attracts us as people and how to deal with the inevitable fear that comes with each transaction.

You'll learn more about why customers ignore you, how to attract (and keep) their attention. You'll discover how to move them through the buying process naturally, without manipulation, coercion or dropping your pants.

Are you ready? Let's get started.

Before we get started...

Visit HooktoWin.com to get access to our Website Wizard. Our Wizard takes you through everything we discuss here, giving you step-by-step checklists, templates and tools you can use for your website.

Part 1

Chapter 1

Alex

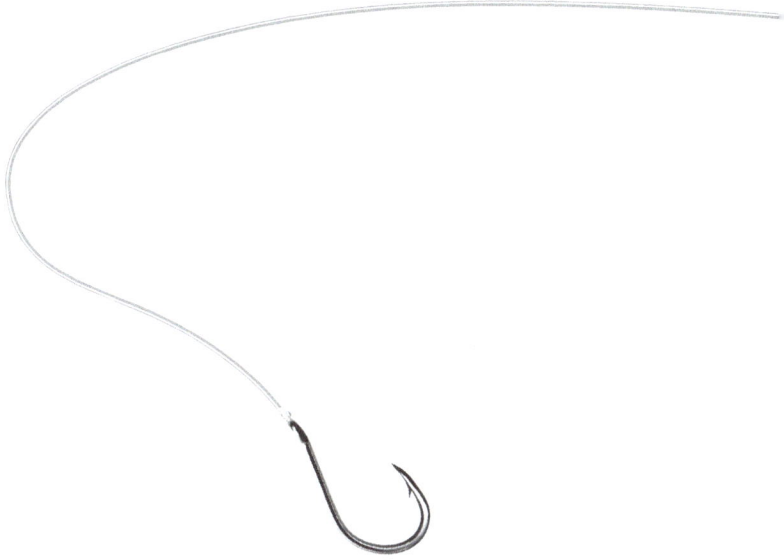

"How could you do this Graham?" Alex shook his head and glared. He hated to think the rumors of Graham & Julie were true, but what was he to think? Graham had been talking about giving Alex this management position for 3 years.

"It's business." Graham responded with a shrug. Alex felt the heat inside him growing stronger. He looked away, his fists and jaw clenched. He couldn't stay. It was the only way for Graham to realize what a big mistake he was making. Alex didn't hesitate. He never did. With one last look around he zeroed in on Graham.

"You're making a mistake." He shook his head. "I quit."

And with a quick turn he went straight to his desk, grabbed his photo of Amy and marched out. Six years. Maybe quitting was a little hasty, but how could Graham have given the promotion to Julie? She had only been here for what? A year and a half?

The sun glared off the windshields of the cars in the parking lot, making it hard to see. That didn't bother Alex because he always parked in the same spot. As he climbed in he thought back to his first day. He had been so ambitious; sure he'd be in management within 5 years. Had he been naïve? Or did he land a job at the wrong company? Alex knew it was unproductive to let his thoughts drift there. But every time he ran into Jason or saw his posts on Facebook he was reminded that while his plan to be in management had failed, Jason was department manager at Harley-Davidson and wouldn't stop bragging about it. Alex shifted into reverse and pulled out of the parking lot. As he sped along I-90 the thought nagged him, *talk to Amy first*. He ignored it. He passed the exit towards home but kept going straight to Paul's house.

We'll start our own business, he thought; his mind racing. Alex didn't stop to consider whether or not Paul would be on board; it was something they'd talked about for years. Anyway, Paul was already doing it as a side business. *No reason we can't make it full time.* They'd need an office, a website, advertising, what else?

Alex let out a deep breath. He felt his excitement rising. He realized he felt lighter.

Alex pulled into Paul's driveway and couldn't get out of the car fast enough. "Paul!" he shouted as he knocked on the door. He heard Paul shout back, "Come in!" And he shot through the door. Paul was sitting at the dining room table wading through a stack of papers. He looked surprised to see Alex and looked at his watch. "Aren't you working right now?"

"Nope," Alex forced himself to slow down and took a seat at the table. He turned to Paul and looked him straight in the face. "I quit my job." He paused briefly and then said "I want to go into business with you, just like we've always talked about." Alex waited earnestly, as confident as he felt earlier he was suddenly unsure how Paul would take the news.

Paul looked confused as he asked, "Wait. What do you mean you quit? What happened?"

Alex explained, "You know the promotion I was waiting for?" Paul nodded. "Graham gave it to Julie." Alex looked at Paul and started to feel defensive. He started to pace. "I had to do it Paul. I just couldn't take it anymore. Obviously the promotion Graham promised me didn't happen, why should I stick around? I want to feel excited again! I want to love what I'm doing." Paul just looked at him. "At least hear me out?" Alex asked.

"Okay, let's hear it then." Paul agreed. He put down the pen he had been holding in his hand and crossed his arms. Doubt nagged Alex's mind. What if he'd made a mistake quitting his job? What if Paul didn't want to do this? He shook it off and made his case. "So I know you've been having a hard time finding a job & you've been trying to do this consulting business. I was thinking I can help. We can do it together. I have more experience with marketing, sales, and business development..." Alex trailed off. "Were you serious all those times in college we talked about having our own business one day? Working together?"

"Does Amy have any idea what's going on?" Paul uncrossed his arms. "Does she know you quit today?" Paul asked. Alex looked down, closed his eyes for a brief moment, and then looked up again at Paul. "I haven't told her yet."

Alex knew Amy would be surprised. He had been so excited about the promotion, he was sure she probably thought it was a done deal. She wanted to have a baby. They had been waiting until he got the promotion. The promotion he was supposed to have gotten today. He sighed. She already stopped taking the pill last month. She was so excited they would be able to start trying for a baby. He knew she was going to be disappointed.

Alex walked over and stood in front of the window. "Paul, I know it's sudden. It's not what we expected. But maybe this is what is meant to happen."

"I was standing there in Graham's office and suddenly everything from the last 6 years became clear. I haven't been happy. I mean, I've been working my ass off trying to earn a promotion to management. But for what? I've always hated working with Graham. I'm tired of all my ideas either being shot down or the credit taken by others. I want to be in control of my own future. Amy wants kids. I want freedom to be in their lives. To come and go when I please."

Alex turned back to Paul. "I think we could be great at this."

Paul picked up one of the stacks of paper he had in front of him. "I'm in the middle of paperwork for my business loan. Talk to Amy, if she's on board we'll get your name on this application as a partner." Alex grinned and jumped up to give Paul a hug.

Paul put his hands up. "Alright, hold up, we still have some things to discuss."

Chapter 2

Amy

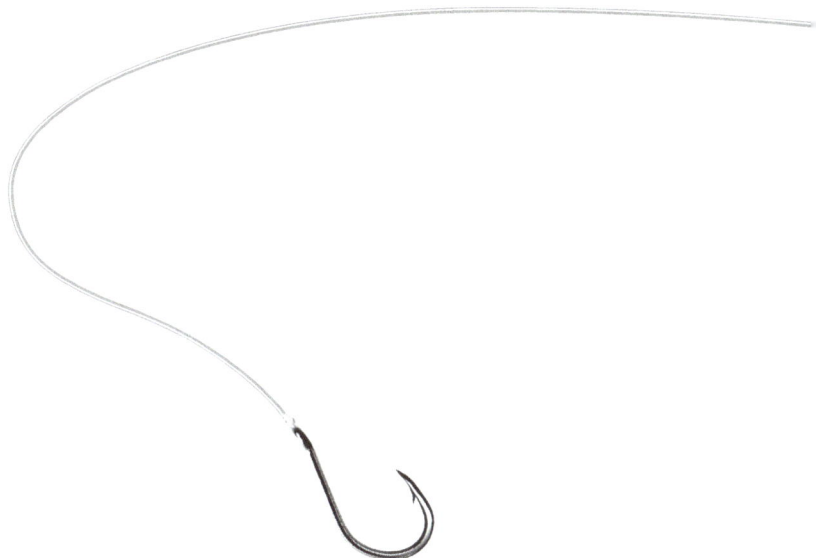

Amy's hands trembled as she worked the wrapper open on a Home Pregnancy Test. She hesitated, wondering if it was too soon. But that's why she bought the 3 pack; she could always wait and test again. She reread the directions, as if she hadn't used one of these before. She worked hard not to get her hopes up. 'Be prepared. It's going to be negative', she told herself. But she couldn't shake the feeling maybe this time was finally different. She wondered how Alex would take it. Oh he wanted children, they talked about that. But she only recently convinced him to agree to stop birth control. Financially things could be better. But Alex would be getting a promotion soon. Didn't he mention that he was meeting with Graham today? Amy's stomach fluttered. She forced herself not to look at the test until the full 3 minutes had passed. It seemed to take an eternity for the numbers on the clock to turn. Okay, she sighed. Here goes.

The anxiety balled up in Amy's stomach moved to her throat as she took a deep breath and finally allowed herself to look. 2 lines. What did 2 lines mean again? Is that positive? Her eyes welled with tears. She grabbed the directions to compare the test stick with the picture. She hadn't made a mistake. 2 lines meant positive. Amy closed her eyes. She was pregnant! She felt the knot in her throat loosen and gave way to more tears.

Amy looked at the clock. Alex would be home in 2 hours. Maybe Graham had finally promoted him today. They had a lot to celebrate! She quickly cleaned up all the evidence. She grabbed a plastic bag from the kitchen, slid the test in and sealed it closed. Then carefully buried the test wrapper in the bottom of the trash where she was sure Alex wouldn't see it. She wanted to surprise him with a special dinner and she didn't want him to expect anything was up if he used the bathroom before dinner. If she hurried she would have enough time to run to the market. She took the box of pregnancy tests and buried it under all her socks.

Her steps were fast and light as she grabbed her purse and did mental calculations of all she would need to pick up at the store. Flowers? Candles? Wine? Wait. No wine. He would wonder why she wasn't drinking. Suddenly she was glad she had prepped a roast in the crockpot this morning.

She stopped at the bakery and picked out one of the gorgeous little 6 inch cakes she had always wanted to get for a special occasion. Chocolate of course. She went through the salad bar; it would save time on prep later. Besides, Alex liked different things on his salad than she did. Deciding against roses, Amy grabbed 3 pillar candles of different sizes to make an arrangement. It had been a long time since they had a candlelight dinner. Had they ever? They would have more now.

She wondered how she would break the news. On the way past the checkout she saw the card aisle. It didn't take long to find the perfect card. Okay, maybe it wasn't perfect but it would work perfectly. It was actually a Thanksgiving card. The front read "Dad" in orange letters with fall leaves and the inside was just a simple message, "I'm thankful for you."

Amy rushed around setting things up as soon as she got home. She finished setting out the food and was in the bedroom pulling her black dress down over her hips when she saw Alex pull into the driveway. She bent over, looked into the mirror and quickly applied some lipstick. She heard Alex at the door and grabbed the card, holding it behind her back with one hand. She skipped out to the living room to meet him. Her large green eyes were sparkling; the dress hugged her body, emphasizing her curves. She was so happy.

Alex looked happy. Amy felt nervous electricity in her stomach that trailed up her arms. She wondered what would be the right moment to tell him. Should she tell him or just hand him the card? She wanted the moment to be special, memorable. *Wait 'til dinner,* she thought. Alex's voice pulled her from her thoughts.

"I have exciting news."

Amy had moved to the table and slid the card under her placemat. She was pouring sparkling grape juice into their goblets. She knew he must be talking about the promotion! She looked up & smiled. "Graham finally …" But Alex held up his hand and cut her off. "Just wait."

"It's probably not what you're expecting but, I just came from Paul's. We were talking about going into business together." Alex paused briefly and put his hands up. "Fifty-fifty. I'll make my own hours, make my ideas count. Be able to do something important. It's the shot I've been waiting for!" Alex looked into Amy's eyes then, and she could see he looked tired; the circles under his eyes deeper than they seemed this morning.

"What do you mean? What happened? Didn't you meet with Graham today? What about the promotion?" Amy's voice trailed off. She didn't know why Alex was talking about going into business with Paul. Her forehead wrinkled in confusion.

"I didn't get it." Alex let out a small sigh. "Julie got it and…."

"I quit." He admitted.

Quit. Suddenly Amy's belly felt heavy & full. She closed her eyes. She wasn't able to gather her thoughts before Alex started talking again. She looked down at her placemat, she thought of the day, of the card she knew was hidden underneath.

"I'm sorry honey. I can see you were expecting to celebrate tonight. Everything looks really nice." Alex looked around at the candles and the food.

"Why didn't you call me?" Amy asked. She wouldn't let herself cry. She started to dish out their food.

Alex nodded his head from side to side "I should have called. But I knew you were going to be disappointed. I thought telling you in person would be better." He kept on.

"But anyway, it's not all bad news. You know Paul & I have talked about working together for years. He's been working on starting his own consulting gig and I talked to him about joining him as a partner, to help him with the business side of things… Amy, he's excited about this; I'M excited about this." Alex started to eat.

Amy decided she wouldn't tell him tonight. Not like this. She picked at her food and poured more juice for herself.

"Amy?"

Amy looked up. Alex must have been talking again. "Yes?"

"I need you to be on board with this. What do you think?" Alex asked.

Amy shook her head. "What do I think? I don't know what I think."

"I mean, this morning you were talking about a promotion. Then you come home and I find out you quit your job? Give me some time to process Alex!" She tossed her napkin down in frustration.

All she could think about was how to get that envelope out from under the placemat without Alex seeing. She had to hide it. She had to wait to tell him. This wasn't how she pictured the night would go.

Chapter 3
Alex

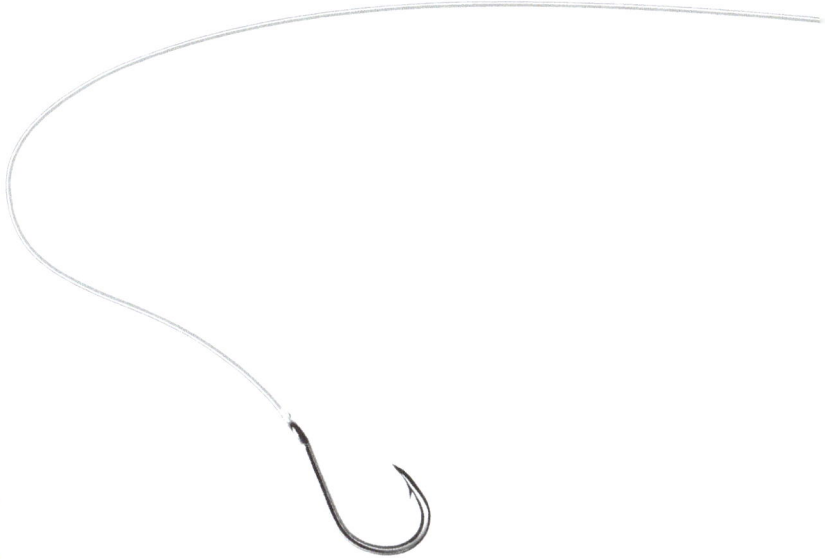

Alex wondered what was going on with Amy. He knew she was disappointed about the promotion, but she had given her support for him to work with Paul. Why had she been distant lately? But he remembered she said she wasn't feeling good and she had been in bed early every day this week. He had been staying up late to work and sleeping past the time when she left for work. They needed to have a date night, spend some time reconnecting.

The smell of brewed coffee spread through the house. Alex finished getting dressed and went to the kitchen. He filled a travel mug with coffee to take with him to Paul's house. As an afterthought he filled a second mug for Paul. He had complained yesterday about his coffeemaker breaking.

Alex slung his computer bag over his shoulder and grabbed the travel mugs. He hoped they would hear back about their business loan today. Paul said not to count on it, since the banker had said it might take as long as Thursday for an answer.

It was a bit overcast outside. Hopefully it would rain. The drive was easy this time of day. Alex thought that starting the day at 10 am had its advantages.

Paul was on the phone when Alex walked in. He motioned for Alex to be quiet and reached out to take one of the travel mugs. "Alright, thank you. You too. Goodbye."

Paul set down his phone and turned to Alex with a big smile. "We're in business!"

They spent the afternoon talking about how to allocate the money. As usual, Paul wanted to take the conservative route.

"I just don't see why we'd need an office right away. We can save money by working from home!" Paul insisted.

"How's that gonna look?" Alex scrunched up his face. "We should look the part. Get an office, furniture, equipment."

"No, I'm telling you we can save money this way. We meet at their office, do conference calls, emails, it's a waste of money to get an office just to 'look the part.' I don't feel comfortable spending on anything that isn't necessary." Paul was adamant.

"Okay." Alex rolls his eyes. "So we get a website up, get advertising going. I know a freelancer we could use. I guess we need to talk about our budget."

"Don't forget we'll have these loan payments to make. I think we need to set aside money to cover the payments." Paul crossed his arms.

"Yeah, I know we're going to have loan payments. But the whole point of seed money is to get us started. We have to take some risks and move forward!" Alex was dumbfounded. They had just applied for a business loan, and they got it. Why did Paul want to just hang on to the money? It didn't make any sense!

"No, I think we hold on to the money for now and just cover the bare minimum expenses. Once we get rolling we can commit to regular advertising."

Alex wanted to punch Paul in the face. What had he gotten himself into? He had always known Paul to be somewhat conservative; he wasn't a risk-taker. Why did Alex think Paul would be different in business? He had been a fool! Now he was on the hook for this loan. He had been so confident about this with Amy. What if it didn't work out?

He left Paul's house feeling frustrated and resentful. Paul had never had to struggle to get where he was in life. He always just expected things to be available, to work out. You would think that would make him more of a risk-taker, but he didn't want to move unless something was a sure thing.

Alex was determined to make this work. If he had to use their personal savings he was going to prove to Paul that marketing and advertising was important in order to get business. No, it wasn't just important, it was *essential* and they needed to budget for that.

Chapter 4

Amy

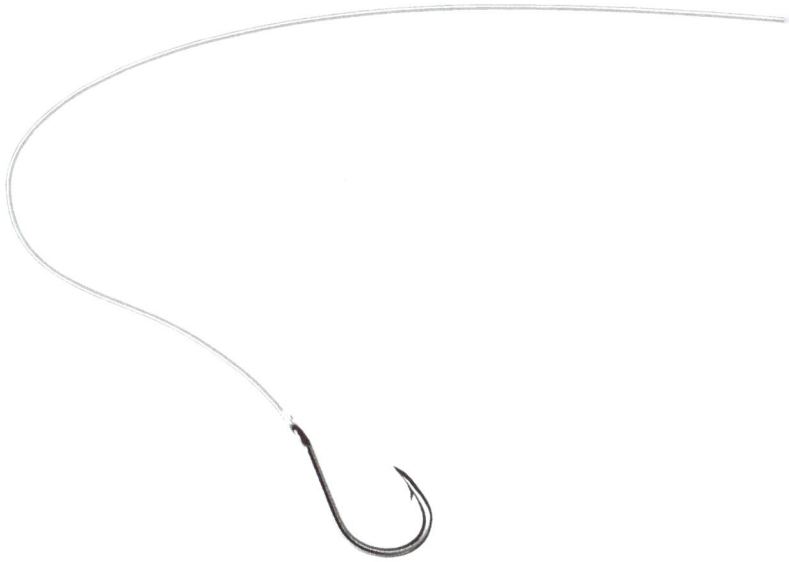

It was Sunday; Amy's favorite day. Alex was still sleeping after another late night spent working. She stepped out of the bathroom into their walk-in closet to get dressed. She knew she wasn't really showing yet, but she felt bloated and her clothes were fitting tighter. Everything was uncomfortable. She hated that her boobs were pushing out over the top edge of her bra. She was surprised Alex hadn't said anything. They were huge! And they hurt.

The longer she waited to tell Alex about her pregnancy the harder it became. He had been so busy with work and it's all he wanted to talk about when she saw him. It was inevitable; she was going to have to tell Alex soon. She had finally called last week to make a Doctor's appointment. They wanted to see her on Friday, she would be 9 weeks then; they asked her if she had been taking her prenatals.

Amy finally ended up putting on a pair of gray sweats and an old college hoodie. She was definitely going shopping today.

She felt lost looking at all the maternity and nursing wear in the mall maternity store. Finally she picked out a couple low rise pants, a belly band, and 4 new bras. The store was busy today and just about everybody seemed ready to check out at the same time. They called for an associate to open up a new register.

"Your total is $158.87," the sales associate said as she finished putting the bras into the bag. Amy swiped her debit card and entered in her pin. "I'm sorry ma'am, it was declined. Do you have another form of payment?" Embarrassed, Amy dug in her purse for her credit card. Why on earth would her debit card be declined? There should be at least $3,000 in there.

When Amy got home she went straight to the computer to log into her online banking. She could hear Alex in the bathroom taking a shower. She waited impatiently for the screen to load. $3.26 *Three dollars twenty six cents!??* She clicked the balance to see a breakdown of transactions. She didn't see anything out of the ordinary at first, just all the regular bills. She kept scrolling. There! $2,000 transferred to PayPal three weeks ago. She went to the bedroom to confront Alex.

"Did you know we only have three twenty six in our checking account? Three *dollars* twenty six cents!?" Amy said, clearly angry.

"You get paid tomorrow though, right? So we should be good."

Alex was hiding something. "Well, either our account was hacked or you have something to tell me because three weeks ago we lost 2 grand to PayPal!" Amy felt exasperated.

"We didn't lose 2 grand to PayPal. I transferred it to my account to cover some business expenses." Alex admitted.

"What business expenses? I don't understand. You said you & Paul got a business loan. Shouldn't that have covered your expenses?" Amy sat down. They clearly hadn't been talking like they should have been.

Alex crouched down in front of Amy and put his hands on her knees. "We needed a website, we needed advertising. Paul was hesitant to spend the loan. He wants to be cautious." Alex stood up and started to pick up some clothes off the floor. "We had a fight about it and I decided to spend my own money on a site." He paused and turned back to Amy. "But it wasn't fair that I didn't talk to you about it first. I was out of line for that and I'm sorry."

"Okay, but we still have some cash in the safe. I'll make a cash deposit later today." Amy said as she moved to go check the safe.

Alex stopped her. "I used some of our cash too."

Amy crossed her arms. "How much?"

Alex grimaced, "Nine hundred."

"Alex! You quit your job! We're living off 1 income and you've blown most of our savings!" Amy felt sick. She ran to the toilet and just made it before she threw up.

"Are you okay babe?" Alex, concerned, handed her a tissue and helped her with her hair.

Amy threw up again.

Then, turning to Alex she blurted, "I'm pregnant."

Chapter 5
Paul

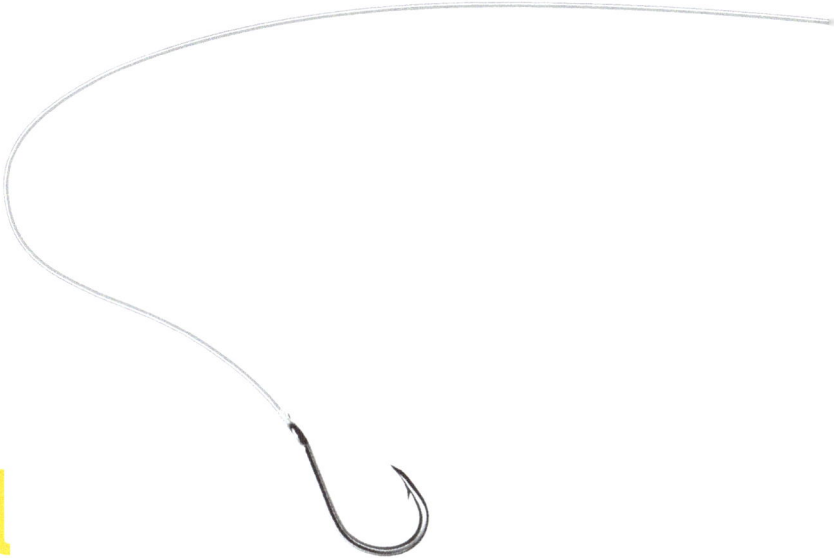

"It's not enough." Paul said as he slunk back in his chair. "We need more money coming in. Even keeping our expenses as low as possible we only have about 3 more months before the loan money is exhausted."

He looked to Alex, "How many leads have you been getting from the website?"

Alex swung his head from side to side. "Eh… not great."

"How many?"

"I don't know."

"How can you not know?" Paul shook his head. "Well, I'd feel more comfortable if you canceled your monthly ads. We need to get some more sales first and then you can go back to advertising."

Alex was frustrated. "Paul, how are we going to get sales without advertising? That doesn't make any sense."

"Word of mouth, networking… I'm checking out a networking group. It's three hundred fifty dollars to join, but that covers membership fees for a year."

"Okay, well, I hope that something works out soon." Alex paused a moment, then admitted. "Amy's pregnant."

"That's not funny." Paul shot back immediately. "Wait, are you serious?"

"Yes I'm serious. How can you think I'd joke about that?" Alex scowled.

"I'm sorry man. Wow. Shit." Paul stood a moment in thought. "I can reach out to people I've worked with in the past, see if anybody needs something."

Paul turns to Alex, "She's still working?"

"Yeah, look Paul, I wasn't trying to freak you out. She's working and I'm sure everything is going to be fine. But you deserved to know." Alex said.

"Thanks for telling me." Paul gave Alex an encouraging smile. "Alright, well we have 3 months. Let's hit it."

Chapter 6

Amy

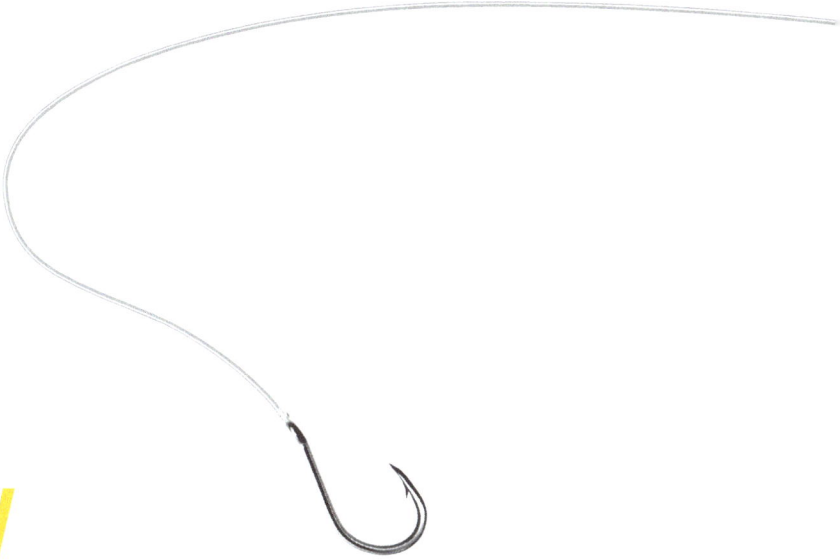

Amy felt nervous as she walked up to the clinic for her Doctor's appointment. Alex was supposed to meet her. She had to work later so her appointment was early. The wait wasn't long and she was called in to speak with a nurse who took her weight, blood pressure, and asked about the date of her last period. Where was Alex? The Doctor came in and asked a bunch more questions and before she knew it Amy was holding her breath while Dr. Breken prepared to listen for a heartbeat. The blue gel was warm as it squirted on to her tummy. She heard what sounded like static and then a heartbeat. "That's your heart there, " Dr. Breken said. "The baby's heart is going to be much faster." She slid the doppler around Amy's stomach a little more until she found the rapid swoosh thump of the baby's heart. In an instant Amy had tears in the back of her eyes. *This is really happening.* She was sad that Alex wasn't there to share the moment with her. She had always dreamed they would hear their baby's heartbeat for the first time together.

There was a quick knock at the door and a nurse came in with a portable ultrasound machine. Dr. Breken said, "Let's take a peek!" Amy smiled and nodded. Dr. Breken squirted some more gel and a moment later Amy was watching the fuzzy black & white images on the ultrasound screen. It was hard to see at first, she didn't know what she was looking at. Then Dr. Breken surprised her. "Congratulations Amy, you're having twins!"

Amy was speechless, she was so shocked. Dr. Breken said the babies looked good but she wanted to schedule a more extensive ultrasound. The rest of the appointment was a blur. She was overwhelmed. She felt happy and scared and worried all at the same time. *Twins!* Alex always said he thought twins would be cool. Amy wondered what he would think now. She wished she didn't have to go to work today, at least it was Friday.

The crisp winter air felt good. A heavy blanket of snow covered everything, fresh from yesterday afternoon. Now, the sun was shining and it made a beautiful picture. Amy was extra careful as she walked out to her car. It was a short, easy drive to work. She hadn't told anyone at work about her pregnancy yet. She wondered when she should. How was this going to work? Pregnant with twins!? She couldn't stop thinking about it. She wondered if she should call and tell Alex, but she was upset he had missed the appointment.

She wasn't at her desk long before she got a call from her boss that he wanted to see her. Her mind was still preoccupied as she sat waiting in his office. He came in with a folder in his hand and sat down. Amy forced herself to pay attention. She didn't particularly love her job, but they needed the income right now. The last thing she wanted to happen was to lose it right now.

"As you know we took a real big hit last quarter, our funding is down by more than 40%, " her boss said. Amy got a feeling this wouldn't end well. A strong feeling of dread poured over her shoulders. She could already feel herself sweating. She braced herself for the worst. And then it came.

"I have to lay you off effective immediately." He handed her the folder. "You're severance check is in there. Molly will be available to help you with any questions you have about continuing your insurance, should you…"

Amy didn't stay to listen to the rest. Without saying a word she stood up and went back to her desk. It took her 5 minutes to clear it off and gather all her stuff. Then she walked out without saying a word. It was only 10:15.

Chapter 7
Alex

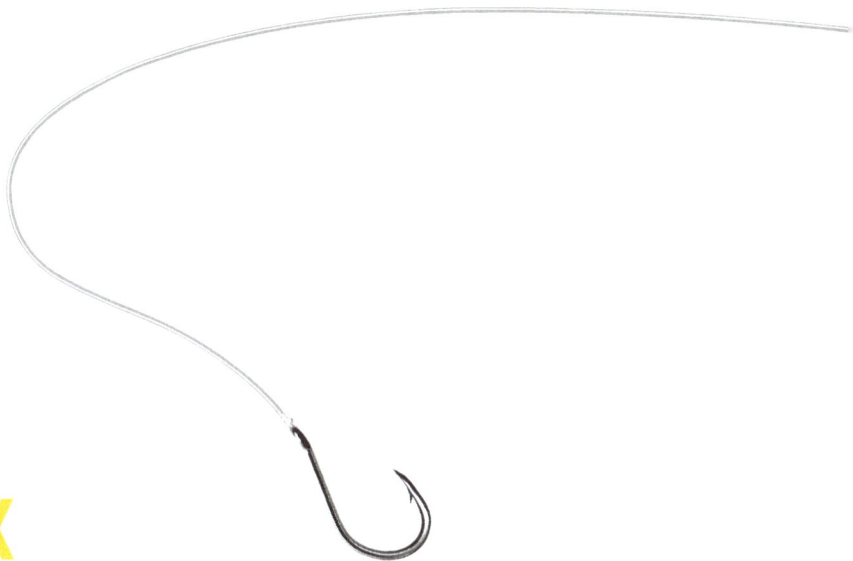

Alex left the house at 5 a.m. for a much needed workout at the gym. He ran 6 miles on the indoor track, and then lifted weights before finishing off in the pool. He didn't usually work out so long but he had been under a lot of stress lately and it was the best way for him to clear his mind.

Things weren't going as well as he'd hoped with the business. It was a lot harder to get going than he thought it would be. They had 2 clients, but those came through referrals. He was frustrated when he thought that maybe Paul was right about the website and advertising. He never should have used their savings for that. But who knows? Maybe things would be worse without the site. At least they looked legitimate online, since Paul didn't want to get an office.

Alex climbed out of the pool and went to the showers. He planned to shower at home but wanted to get the chlorine off before he changed back into his sweats.

It was 8:37 when he got back to their apartment. He was hungry so he popped a bagel in the toaster; he went to the fridge to grab the cream cheese and orange juice when he saw it. Amy's first Doctor's appointment was today at eight. He had missed it! He felt awful. He went to his phone. He saw a text from Amy at 8:06. *Where r u?*

He called Amy but she didn't pick up. He called Paul, who picked up on the 2nd ring.

"Paul, can you reschedule our meeting..." Alex started before Paul cut him off. "Don't worry about it, I got a message from Jon they want to move the meeting to Monday because he wants Jesse to be there too."

"Okay, great. That works out then, "Alex said, relieved. "I'm going to take off the rest of the day; maybe do some stuff from home. So I'll see you Monday okay Paul?"

"Alright, see you Monday." Paul said.

Alex jumped in the shower. He would surprise Amy at work and take her out to lunch and hear about how the appointment went. He felt bad that he had missed it but he would be sure to go to the next one. He knew he had to make it up to her. He had really been screwing up lately.

After his shower he worked on the dishes and put a load of clothes in the washer. It was still only eleven. He shrugged; they could make it an early lunch.

He grabbed his keys and wallet and put his coat on. He debated over whether to order takeout and surprise her with it, or just go pick her up and they could go somewhere together. He decided to surprise her and that way she could choose the restaurant. They hadn't done lunch together in a while. He was looking forward to it. He kept trying her on her cell but it was going straight to voicemail.

When he got to her office at 11:15 he didn't see her car. He waited awhile, thinking that maybe she was out running an errand for her boss. Amy worked for a non-profit organization. They served youth and underprivileged and she helped run their summer day camp. This time of year they would be busy planning for the coming summer.

It was 11:24 and there was still no sign of her car. He decided to go and wait for her inside and find out where she went. He was approaching the door when one of Amy's coworkers, Tina, came out. Alex smiled, "Hi Tina, where's Amy? Do you think she'll be back soon?" Tina looked surprised.

"Oh! Didn't she call you?"

"No..." Alex was puzzled. What was going on? Why was Tina acting so weird?

"I hate to be the one to tell you. It doesn't seem right. But... she was laid off this morning." Tina admitted.

Alex felt the weight of her words like a ton of bricks hitting him in the face. *Amy lost her job. Why hadn't she called him? Where was she?* He mumbled a quick goodbye Tina and turned back to his car. He had to find Amy.

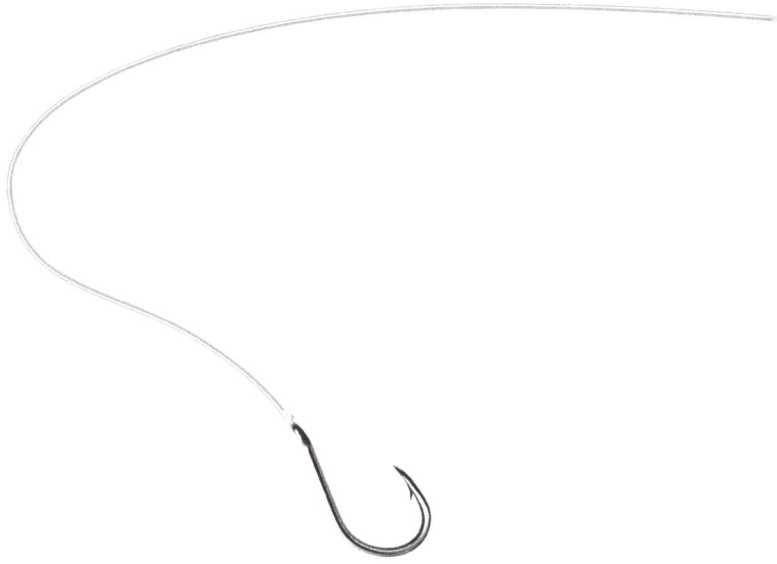

Chapter 8

Amy

Amy had been wandering around Babies R Us for about an hour. She sat down in a glider rocker and put her feet up. She felt sad and she wished she felt different. She wanted to be over the moon about having twins. But all she felt was overwhelmed and scared. How were they going to do this? She looked up and suddenly Alex was there, next to her, in a navy recliner. Her eyes filled with tears and she smiled weakly. It was comforting to see him. She should have called him; how did he find her?

"I lost my job."

He reached out and grabbed her hand. "I know."

Amy was reminded again how much she loved this man. She laughed. "We're having twins." And she looked at him and cried. "What are we gonna do now?"

Chapter 9

Alex

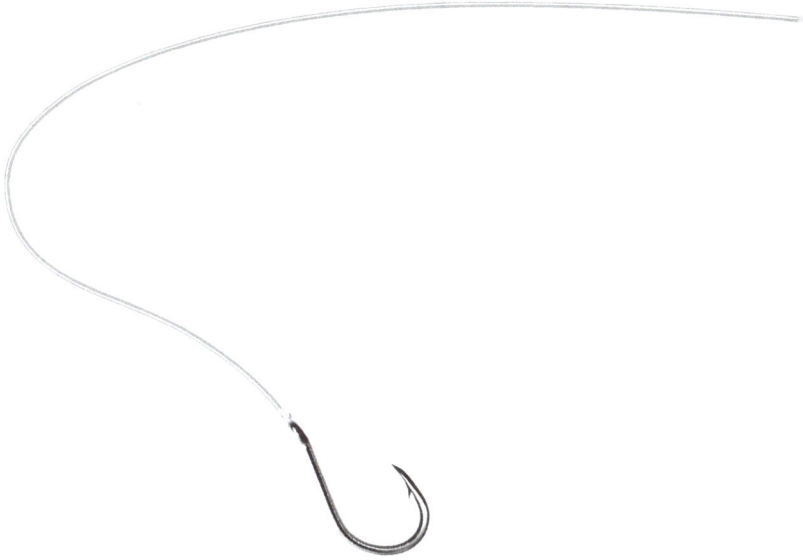

Amy's words echoed through Alex's mind. *"We're having twins."* He was excited about the babies, but worried too. They were in a really tight spot now. The lease on their apartment was up for renewal. And now with him and Amy both out of work it was going to be tough to make it. He wished he hadn't spent so much on the AdWords campaign; they had only gotten 1 lead from all that. What a waste! Their savings account was almost completely drained. How they were going to get what they needed to take care of twins he had no idea!

Monday morning Alex drove to Paul's house. He dreaded the conversation he was to have but it couldn't be helped. Amy was right. They had to stop hiding things.

Alex could tell that Paul sensed something was up. He just stood and looked at Alex, waiting to hear what was going on.

"I've got good news and bad news." Alex said.

Paul braced himself. "Okay, bad news first, let's hear it."

Alex took a deep breath and sighed. "Well, Amy was laid off Friday. Same day she found out she's carrying twins, by the way, and Saturday we got notice from our landlord about our lease and they are increasing our rent by $100/month. We have to make a decision and get back to them; if we don't want to renew our lease we'll have to move out, obviously." Alex sighed again and ran his fingers through his hair. "We can't renew our lease Paul, what are we gonna do?"

"Aaaaaagh!" Paul groaned. "When things are tough they just get tougher, don't they?"

Then Paul started to laugh and shake his head. "I'm sorry man; I know it's not funny. Just wow. This business thing is harder than I thought. You have great ideas and you think you're going to do something great, then life and reality shows up and surprise! Figure this out, slick."

Alex just stood with his arms crossed over his chest and waited for Paul to finish. He hadn't expected this reaction. He wasn't sure what he expected, but he didn't think he would laugh.

"Okay, okay, I'm sorry." Paul calmed down. "How much time do you have until your lease is up?"

"Seven weeks." Alex responded.

"I've got lots of room here. You guys move in here with me until we get this business on its feet and you can get your own place." Paul offered.

Alex hesitated. "I don't know, are you sure?" He knew Paul had the room; this was his parents' house. They had left it to him and his sister when they died, but his sister lived downtown.

"Absolutely! It's paid off, utilities & taxes, that's all we have to worry about. It makes the most sense, don't worry about it. Talk to Amy and figure it out."

Paul turned and looked at Alex, "Twins?" He smiled and shook his head. "Wow, way to go... congratulations man! Was that the good news?"

Alex smiled. "No, I was going to tell you I heard back from that guy that contacted me through the website. We have a meeting Thursday."

"That's great news! Let's hope there is more where that came from huh? God knows we don't have much time to turn this around."

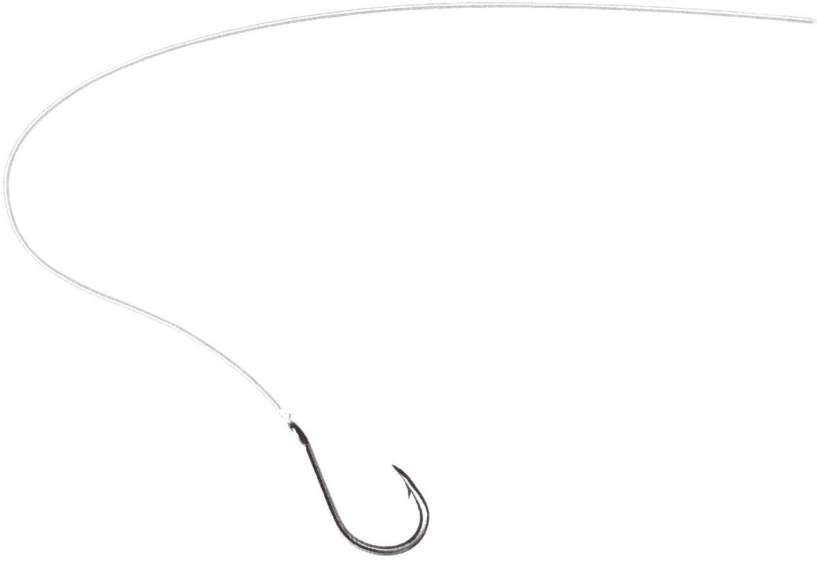

Chapter 10
Amy

It was moving day. Alex wouldn't let Amy do much of anything. She was frustrated but she knew it was best for the babies. She was thankful for Paul's offer to live in his parent's old house. At just under two thousand square feet it had 4 bedrooms, 2 baths, office, living, dining room, and kitchen. She was thankful they wouldn't be cramped. Still, they took out a storage unit for their furniture, since Paul's place was already furnished. It was a beautiful house, but she wished things were different. She had always imagined she would be decorating a nursery in a home of their own. Would she even have a nursery? Her thoughts got away with her as they drove another load over to the house.

"Are you worrying again?" Alex asked. Amy smiled and rolled her eyes. "Trying not to, but not doing the best job."

"How are you holding up?" Amy asked Alex.

"With moving I'm fine I guess. I mean, it's definitely not ideal but it does take some stress off the situation. Remember that networking group that Paul joined?"

"Yeah."

"Well, he was so sure that it would be an easy way to get some business. Hopefully it gets better because so far everything I've done has been a waste of my time. Everybody wants free information, free help, nobody wants to buy." Alex sighed. "It's just getting really old."

"On top of that, the money from the business loan is just about gone. So we're getting more desperate and I hate that. I don't like feeling as if I'm desperate and I have to beg people to work with us. It's pathetic."

"I thought you guys had a few clients you were working with?" Amy asked, puzzled.

"Yeah, well those are both clients Paul brought in when he started. We aren't doing much for them right now. I guess that's the downside to a consulting gig. It doesn't appear to be that consistent." Alex pulled into the driveway of Paul's house. *Their house.*

"Sweetie, I really don't want you to be worrying." Alex pushed the release on his seatbelt and reached over and wrapped his arms around Amy. He kissed the top of her head and leaned down to kiss her growing belly. He spoke to her tummy, "I love you babies." Amy's belly was a cute little bump and not uncomfortable to move or get around yet.

Alex sat up and opened his door. "I have another meeting with Alan next week. He's been dragging his feet for the last 5 weeks. He seems to want to work with us but I'm not sure why he's hesitating to get started."

"I'll be praying special about it. I hope it comes through." Amy said.

Alex smiled. "Me too, babe."

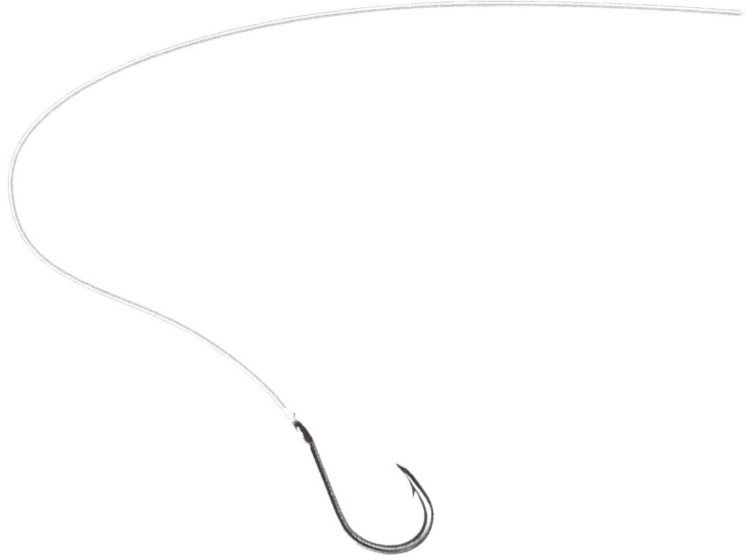

Chapter 11
Paul

Paul couldn't wait for the weekend. Alex and Amy were supposed to be gone visiting family; He wanted some quiet time. It's not like they were too loud or anything; but he did hear them arguing from time to time, and that was awkward. Amy had always been a bit messy, or so Alex said. Lately she was worse, moping around and not doing much besides sleeping, eating, and watching TV. He was annoyed every time he went to rinse his breakfast bowl the sink was already full of dishes and he couldn't get at the faucet. Paul was sure she was depressed. Alex reminded him that the pregnancy hormones made things tough for her. Still, he hoped things with the business would improve soon so things could start to turn around.

He had been busy lately, but cash flow was still a real problem. He wasn't one to panic, but the situation was definitely troubling. He sat at his desk and sorted through the newest stack of mail. He dreaded this task. He had a feeling he already knew what he would find; that they had run out of cash and would not be able to pay their bills. Paul was relieved they hadn't signed an office lease. What a mess that would have been! As it stood the biggest liability they were carrying was the business loan.

After going through the numbers Paul sat back in his chair and sighed. It was just as he thought. He wrote out a check for their loan payment. It was all he could pay. They would have to put off paying for everything else until they could get some more cash. He wondered if he should be considering getting a temp job or something. *Just wait 'til you hear back from Alex.*

Alex was out meeting with Alan, again. Paul hoped the guy would end their misery. *Just sign up or forget it already!*

Finally, the phone rang. Paul picked up, his stomach tied in knots, waiting to hear the news.

Alex voice came through on the line. "He signed."

Paul let out a whistle. "Wheew! Yes, finally!"

"I'm headed to the bank with his deposit now."

Chapter 12

Alex

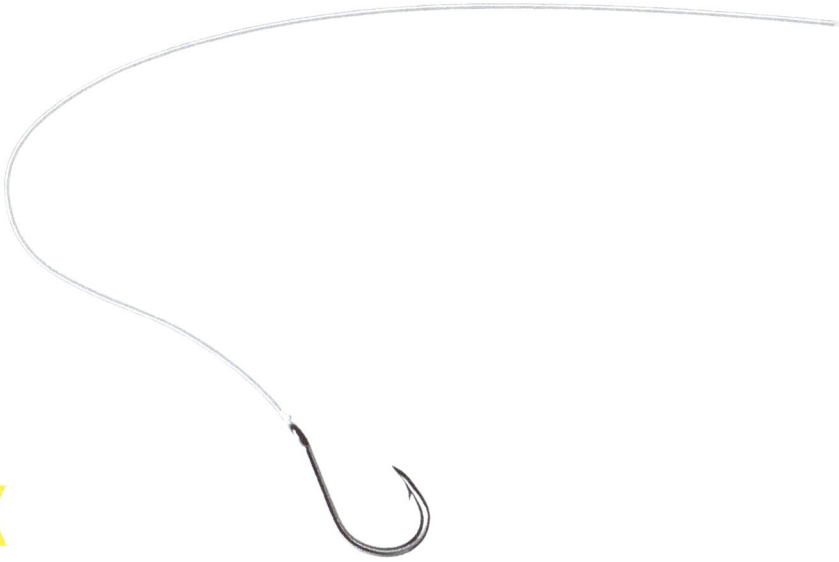

It had been a month since they had signed with Alan. He had turned out to be difficult to work with, but Paul had been putting in extra hours to get the job done. Amy was on bed rest now, so Alex worked almost exclusively from home to be near to help her when she needed it. He did meetings via phone conference and Skype. Paul did all the traveling and onsite work.

Alex had a feeling today was going to be tough. He had just gotten a text from Paul saying the charge for Alan's next payment didn't go through. So he had to deal with that. To top it off, Alan had sent an email late last night demanding a bunch of changes. Alex figured the best thing to do was call him and try to figure it out.

"Alan, it's Alex calling. A couple things, your payment for your latest invoice didn't go through. Do you have a different card we should use?"

"No, I'm not paying it. I told Paul he needs to come up with something else. Your plan is garbage. I've been doing this for years, you were still in diapers when I started this business. I know what works. You need to do it my way and I expect the results you promised when you sold me on working with you."

Alex was taken off guard by Alan's response. He had kind of gotten the feeling that Alan was unhappy from his email last night but he really didn't expect for him to refuse to pay them.

"Look Alan, you hired us to consult on this. If you're not willing to trust our recommendations I'm not sure what we can do. It doesn't make sense that we would do it your way and guarantee the results. We can only guarantee our own work."

"I want my money back then." Alan said.

"We've already done the work. We aren't going to give a refund for work you asked for just because you've now changed your mind." Alex responded, exasperated.

"You're fools! Do you think you can get away with this? You'll be hearing from my lawyer. You're going to wish you had done what I asked the first time." Alan shouted and hung up the phone.

Alex shook his head and sat back in disbelief. *What a piece of work. Nothing he was saying made any sense.*

Chapter 13
Paul

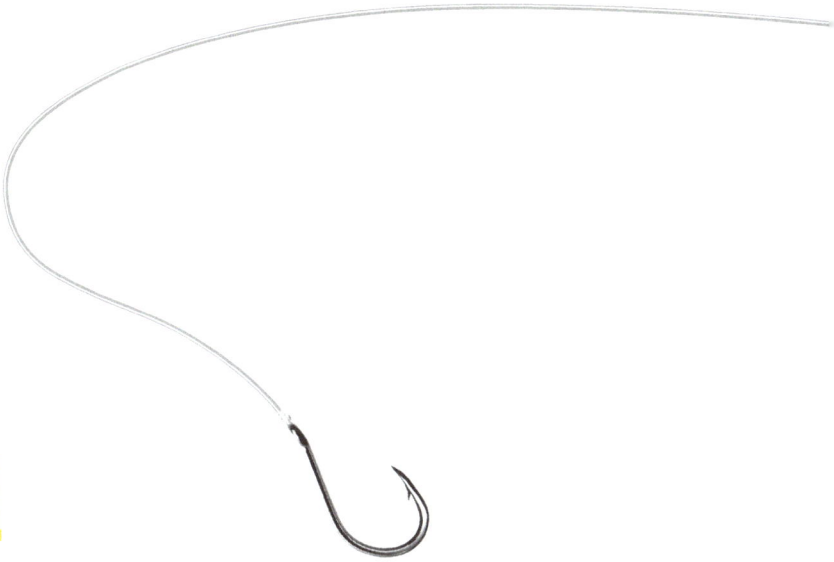

Paul met his sister Jess for lunch. It had been months since they'd seen each other. They had both been so busy, Paul couldn't even remember if he had told her about Alex and Amy moving in. He felt bad asking her for money when they had been so out of touch, but few options remained at this point. The business loan was in danger of default. He felt so angry. He blamed Alan. He had thought the job was the start of things turning around; instead it ended up being a nightmare. They had sunk in extra hours trying to fix things and make it right and it made no difference. He wasn't happy, and now he wouldn't pay.

Jess arrived. She set her purse on the table and kissed him. "Hello baby brother, so good to see you!" She smiled and sat down. "It's been too long, how are you doing? How is your business?"

Paul hesitated. Jess read him right away. "Oh honey, what's wrong?" She was eight years older than him and had always babied him. He was almost sure she wouldn't refuse her help with a loan, but he was nervous anyway.

"I can't help if I don't know what's going on." Jess urged.

"I hate to ask, but I'm in a real bad spot. I need to borrow some money." Paul finally said.

Jess leaned forward, her forehead wrinkled in concern. "What's going on? What happened?"

"Our loan is in danger of default. We've been struggling to get customers. We have a few regulars, but they're not bringing in enough cash flow. Amy lost her job. She's five months pregnant with twins by the way; she's on bed rest, and they moved into the house with me about 8 weeks ago. We've been doing a bunch of different things to try and get leads but we're just really having a tough time. Alex signed a new client about a month ago but he turned into a nightmare, the guy's unhappy and wants to sue for a refund because he changed his mind about what he wanted. So, as you can imagine he's no longer paying us either."

Paul sighed; he knew he needed more than just a loan. He needed her marketing expertise. She helped people figure out how to grow their businesses for a living. "I know we can't really afford you, and I don't know how long it would take me to pay back the loan, but if we have any hope of surviving we need your help, sis."

"Please show us what to do to get more customers." Paul asked.

Jess thought a moment before she answered. "I can help you with your loan payments. I want to make sure your business loan stays out of default. As for help with getting customers and growing your business, I'm also happy to help with that but I will only do so on the condition that you guys put in the effort and do what I say to fix things and set things up properly."

Paul sighed in relief. "Absolutely! We'll do whatever it takes."

"What is the first step?" He asked.

Jess looked at her schedule on her tablet. "We sit down together as soon as possible. We need to get started right away. Are you available tomorrow at 8?"

Paul laughed, "Anytime. Yes, absolutely."

Chapter 14

Alex

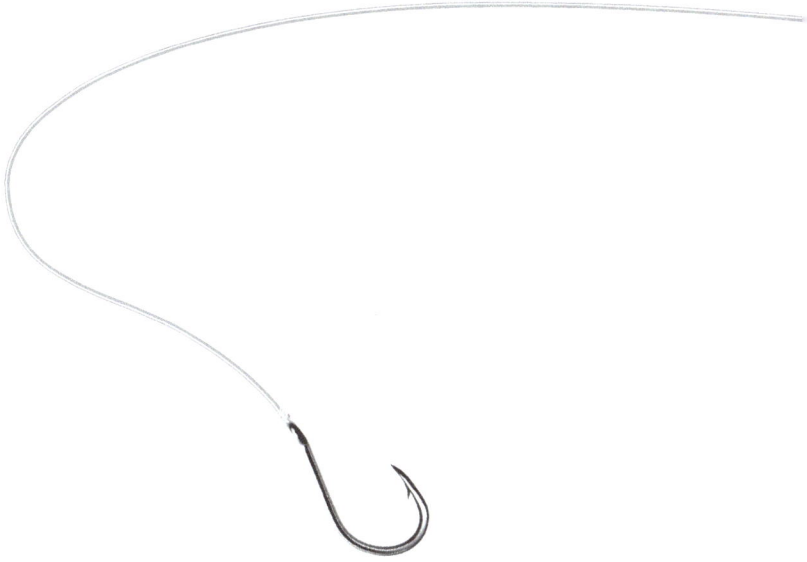

Alex felt thankful that Paul's sister Jess was going to help them make the payments on the business loan, but he wasn't sure how he felt about the terms and conditions. How was he to know that Jess really knew what she was doing? She came over at 8 a.m. like she said she would, and she didn't waste any time. She was intense.

"I need to see everything you've got. Marketing materials, website, sales copy, emails, anything you're currently using or have used in the past to help you get your customers—I need to see it. I also have a bunch of questions I'm going to need you to think about and answer. I need to know how much you've spent on your advertising and what kind of returns you've been getting so far. Please take your time in answering these questions; they will help me come up with a better plan of action." Jess handed each of them a worksheet and then looked at her watch.

"I am going to need everything back to me by 6 p.m. tonight so I can get started. Now, I have got to go to a meeting, so I'll leave you with this, Paul." With a kiss on the cheek she handed Paul a check. And just like a whirlwind, she was gone.

Paul looked at Alex and smiled. "Think she knows what she's doing yet?"

Alex shook his head and smiled. "She's got the confidence, that's for sure."

Chapter 15

Amy

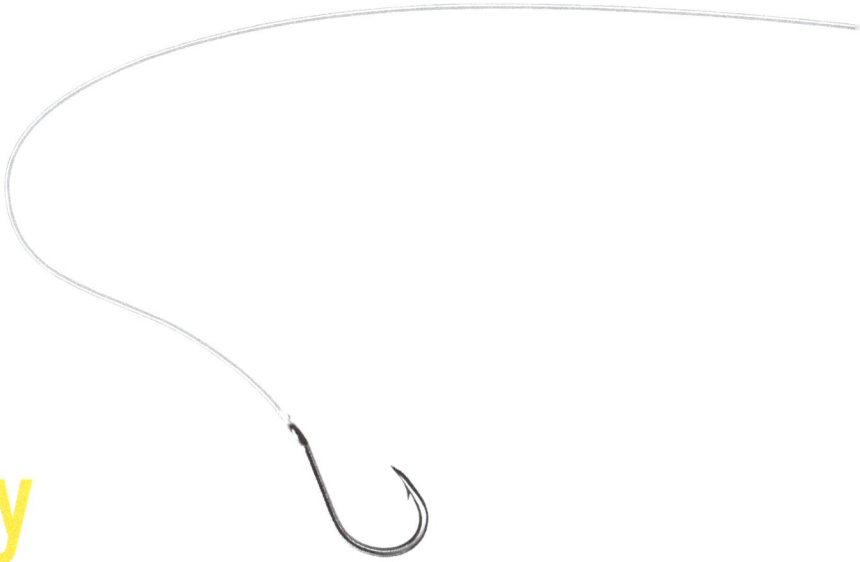

Bed rest was driving Amy stir crazy. All the visions she had of a cute growing belly, of shopping and decorating a nursery, going for walks with Alex, maybe taking one last trip together before the baby came, nothing about her dreams of pregnancy had come true. She was depressed and she knew it. She spent the days reading or watching TV, eating, and trying to sleep. She also spent a considerable amount of time online, looking at online baby shops adding things to their baby registry. She was sick of being stuck at home in bed or on the couch. Alex had been so busy working they had hardly seen each other. She was lonely.

Amy sent Alex a text. *How's it goin?* She waited for a reply but he didn't respond. She tossed her phone down and put her hands over her face, then turned and hugged the blankets on the bed, trying to find a comfortable position. She had to pee, again. She got up and waddled carefully to the bathroom. Paul had given them the master suite when they moved in so she didn't have to go far.

After using the toilet she grabbed her laptop. She wasn't tired anyway. She continued her research on car seats. There were so many to choose from, and everyone had different opinions about features. There were safety ratings to consider, price, and color. Alex wanted something neutral but she loved the cutesy ones. She wished they knew the sex of the babies. They hadn't cooperated during the ultrasound and the tech wasn't able to get a good view.

She was browsing through crib sets when Alex came in. He looked exhausted. "How ya doin babe? I'm sorry I didn't get your text until just now. I've been scrambling to get everything together for Jess." Alex said.

"What's her plan?" Amy asked as she closed the lid on her laptop.

"Honestly, I don't know yet. She didn't go into it, just told us to get her all this stuff by 6 o'clock tonight."

Amy was so tired and overwhelmed with everything. She erupted. "Alex, you have 2 children on the way! We need stuff to take care of them! I don't know why you're wasting your time anymore on this business. It's just not working; I don't understand why you can't just let it go and move on."

"Look, sweetie, I understand you're upset. I know. I get it. I just can't let this go yet." Alex came and sat down next to her on the bed. "We have so much at stake here. How can you ask me to give up when we're so close?"

"How can you say you're close? How do you know this is going to work?"

"I don't know. You're right, I don't really know what will happen." Alex admitted. "But I know what will happen if we quit now. Paul could lose this house, for one. We'd still have the same problems we have now, two babies on the way and no income. I'd have to find a job, and that could take a while, we don't know." Alex shook his head. "But what if this does work? Jess seemed so confident. And Paul believes in her."

"Of course he does, she's his sister!" Amy shot back.

"Look, she knows what she's doing. She's given Paul money to cover our loan payments while we fix this and get back on track. I'd be a fool to not try and give this another shot." Alex insisted.

"Well Alex, I sure hope you're right about this because I can't take much more." And with that, Amy got up to draw herself a bath.

Chapter 16
Alex

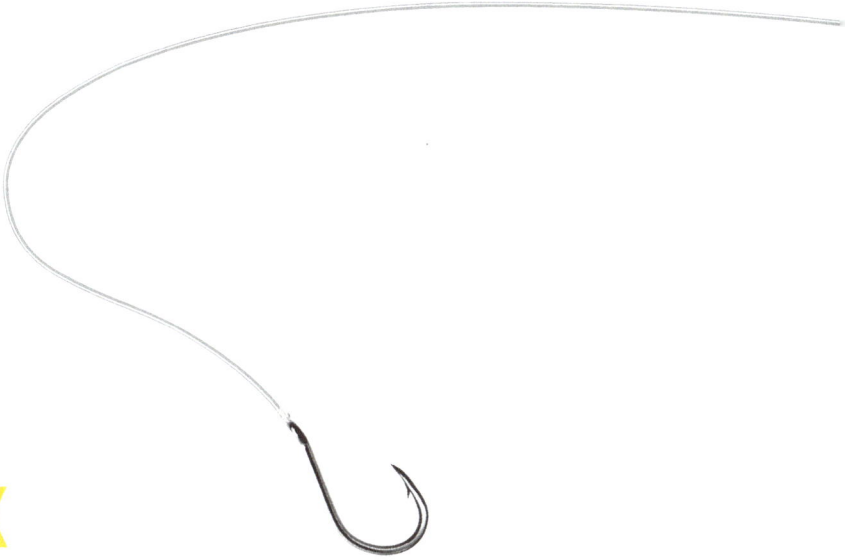

Alex leaned back in his chair. His head was spinning with everything Jess had been telling them. Their site was lacking personality, they weren't communicating clearly, concisely, or effectively. How is it that Alex had worked in sales for 6 years and he had never heard most of what Jess was explaining to them?

"Look, Alex, think of it this way, if you were shopping for a minivan for Amy and the kids, what would you be looking for? What would catch your attention? Do you educate yourself on your options? What attracts you to one vehicle over the other?" Jess asked.

"Are you sure you don't just go along with what Amy picks out Alex?" Paul joked.

Alex smiled at Paul then looked back to Jess and nodded. "I think I get where you're going."

"Yes, you always start with a problem. In this case, the problem is a need. So you have a need, what do you start doing?"

"Shopping."

"And how does someone shop? Remember, everyone is different so what draws you won't necessarily draw me. Some are fascinated by mystery, some passion, others alarm or rebellion, some people are looking for a trusted brand, product or service. Others are drawn to power or confidence, and some are status seekers that want luxury and prestige. Whatever values you have will shape the products and services you are interested in as well as the advertising that pulls you in." Jess adds a bright blue book with the word *Fascinate* to the stack of resources she has shared with them. "You'll want to read this one too."

Then she turned back to Alex. "So what are you looking for in a vehicle for Amy?"

"Something safe, reliable. We've actually had our eye on the Honda Odyssey." Alex responded.

"Okay, think about what attracts you to that minivan over the others."

"Well, I've heard good things, I like the ratings." Alex wasn't sure how to respond.

"It sounds like trust is really important to you. You want a trusted brand and a trusted product. Does that sound right?" Jess asked.

"Yeah, that sounds right."

"So, think about how you came to the conclusion that Honda was trustworthy. You probably did a bunch of reading. Maybe you have positive past experiences with the brand. There are a thousand little things that contribute to your confidence in the choices you make. You just don't consciously realize all that goes into the influencing of your choices."

Jess went on. "Let's recap. You're in business because your clients have a problem and you're service is to help them solve that problem, or problems." She paused briefly and smiled. "You grab their attention when you communicate from an angle that triggers their interest. Everything about how you communicate is important in presenting yourself in an authentic way. Consider all your communication to be your packaging. I mean everything. From your customer service down to the design, typography, and layout of your website and marketing materials, you are presenting your personality and communicating something about your business to the client. Are you professional? Are you informed? Are you reliable, credible?"

Jess paused again and asked, "Are you with me?"

Paul and Alex nodded.

"So you've got their attention. So what? How can you get them to come closer? You're looking to attract them, not just get them to notice you."

Jess had already gone over this. She tested them. "What do you do?"

"You said before that education attracts." Paul answered.

"Yes, now tell me how and why you provide education." Jess probed.

Alex cleared his throat and referenced his notes from earlier. "We can use any form of content to educate. It gives us credibility in the client's eyes." He paused then added, "You also talked about communicating in terms that matter to the client, that it should be more about them and what they need and want and less about us."

Jess smiled. "Okay, so now I'm going to pick on you a bit, baby brother." She winked at Paul. "Imagine two lonely people. Their problem is that they're alone. But they can solve that problem for each other right?" She paused and started drawing on a piece of paper. "Remember the problem comes first right?"

"Right." Paul said.

"You see a girl and something about how she looks catches your attention. C'mon, you know everyone has a type, right? It's your trigger of attraction. But what if you see what you think is a beautiful girl but then you overhear her acting outright nasty to the people she is with? Not so attractive anymore, right?" Jess continued to draw on the sheet of paper. "Contrast the bitchy girl with someone sweet, fun, great sense of humor, intelligent. You've heard the term, the whole package, right? Of course! So, all the messages that are communicated through appearance, actions, words, these are all part of the package. When you spend time getting to know the girl, you are becoming educated on who she is and what she can add to your life."

"I hope this metaphor is making sense." Jess went on. "In life and in business, when you're close to making a choice you start to get anxiety. You aren't sure you're ready to make a commitment. Before you're ready to commit you want to get more personal, right? You want to know more about the other person. You now start to care about their background."

"Once you've attracted clients and they've qualified themselves, they will want more information, good, solid information about you. Just like you, Paul, wouldn't be interested in dating a girl that won't let you get at who she really is. You want to be sure you're presenting yourself as you really are to your clients. Your dream girl should be interested in the real you. Your clients are not worth your time if they are put off by who you are. It's not personal, but we all know not everybody or every situation is going to be a good match for each other. Do yourself a favor and don't be afraid to be authentic." Jess stopped and asked, "Is this metaphor working?"

"I think so, I'm following." Paul nodded and smiled. "Go on."

"So we're at conversion. You're going to come to a call to action, don't be afraid to ask for the date! Think yes and yes. Try giving her two different options for going out with you. Would you like to go to a movie or meet for coffee?" Jess scripted.

"And don't forget, keep things relevant! You don't want to create friction by offering irrelevant information. Don't distract from getting to the action you're looking for." Jess winked at Alex then looked at Paul. "Remember the rule of consumption. In this example, the more you date, the more dates you have."

"Hey, I *am* dating!" Paul laughed and put up his hands.

"Okay, okay…" Jess trailed off. "So, back to business, a great example of a company doing an excellent job creating urgency to increase conversions is Threadless. They sell a limited amount of each artist's design and once it's sold out, it's gone, unless there is enough demand for a reprint. So as a consumer, if you miss out on getting your size, you're out of luck until they do a reprint. And even then, you still have to place your order before they sell out again! So there is definitely a sense of urgency and that is built in to their business model."

They talked until after 11 p.m. until Jess was convinced they understood all the concepts she was trying to teach them. Alex and Paul had a list of things they needed to do and a rough plan laid out for how they would transform their business. Amy was sleeping when Alex climbed into bed. His whole body ached; he was exhausted. Still, his mind kept rolling through everything they had discussed. He finally drifted to sleep to the steady sounds of Amy's pregnancy snore.

Chapter 17

Paul

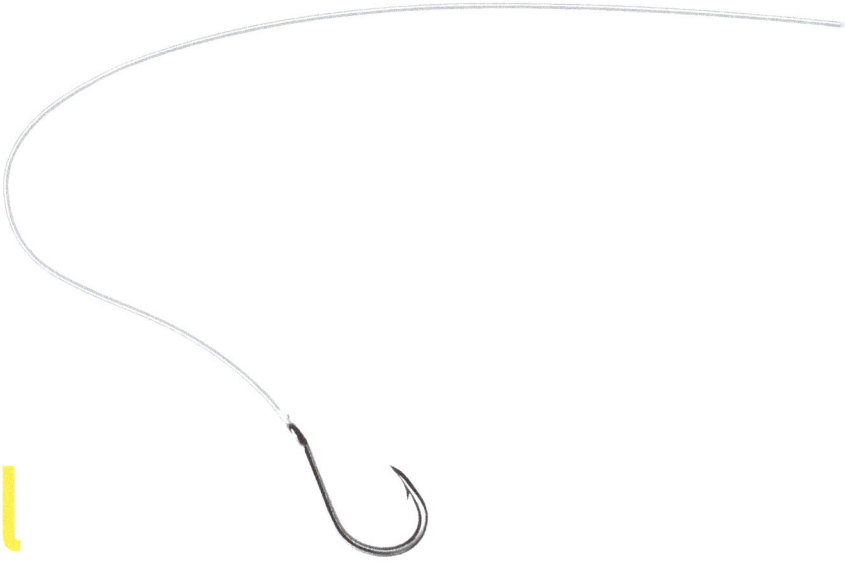

Paul felt energized after the meeting with Jess. He wished he had approached her for help sooner. Maybe they would have avoided this mess in the first place. When they started, Alex had seemed to think he would have no problems with marketing and sales, but they had come to learn that being responsible for generating your own leads was no easy task. Or rather, it could be easy, under the right set up. They definitely did not set things up properly. But now, thankfully, with help from Jess, they were prepared to re-launch their business and ad campaigns and start to generate more qualified customers.

Paul appreciated that his sister was generous enough to cover their business loan payments and he didn't want to abuse her help so he and Alex had worked 60 and 70 hour weeks coming up with new content and ad copy. They were also fortunate that her boyfriend had agreed to do them a favor by redesigning their website and print materials.

"Alex, check it out, Nick made the site live!" Paul said, excitedly.

Alex whistled. "Now that's sharp."

Paul shook his head. How he wished they hadn't wasted their money doing all the wrong things in the beginning. "Looks like we're going to owe Nick and Jess one heck of an engagement gift." Paul said at last.

"Damn straight!"

"Wait, are they engaged?" Alex asked.

"They will be soon; Nick talked to me about it last week." Paul answered with a grin. He reached in his back pocket for his wallet and got out the business AMEX card. He tossed it to Alex. "Here. Let's give this a go. Get those ads running!"

Chapter 18
Alex

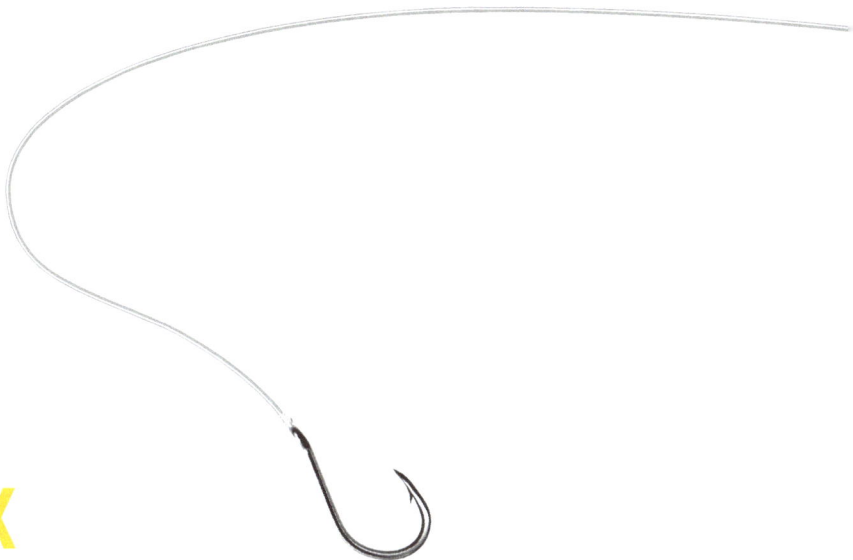

Alex knew how badly Amy had longed to have a baby, and he felt bad things had been so tough for them during her pregnancy. In between all the work he had been putting in to re-launch the business, he had made arrangements to surprise her with a baby shower. Her friend and ex-coworker, Tina, had been happy to help. She had decorated Paul's dining room in a red, aqua, and white motif. There were tissue poms hanging from the ceiling. The fare was simple, fresh fruit, appetizers, punch, and cake.

Amy mingled and visited with all their guests. She was beautiful in a simple, black, form fitting maternity top and full panel maternity jeans. Her stomach was full and round. Alex shook his head as he looked around at all the gifts and the people. He was touched by the obvious generosity of their guests. The gift table was full and overflowing, on top and underneath.

He declined to participate in the activities and the gift opening, preferring instead to watch Amy's joy as she unwrapped the boxes, two of everything. *He was about to have 2 babies –twins! What had they gotten themselves in to?* She was happy. It was plain to see.

Paul motioned for him to step back into the office. Alex followed him in.

"It's working!" Paul exclaimed.

"Check this out."

"You just couldn't resist, could you?" Alex smiled as he bent down to look at Paul's screen. He had shut his phone off for the party. Their ads had been live for a week and they had been checking multiple times every day, waiting for the response they were hoping for. "Alright, we're at 3 downloads and… Woah! *Seven* email subscribers?"

"Now check your email." Paul waited.

Alex saw an email from someone named Derek Steingarton. He read aloud. *"Please contact me, I'm interested in speaking to you about some work I need."*

"Alright!" Alex laughed and turned to give Paul a hug. "We'll call him tomorrow!"

Chapter 19
Amy

The last few weeks had passed quickly. Amy's Sister, Sharon, had stayed for a week after the shower and was only too happy to help wash, sort through, and set up all the baby clothes and items they had received as gifts. They chatted as they sorted the clothes and carefully folded them into bins labeled by size. They opted to leave the cribs in the boxes, and debated about whether to assemble the changing table right away or not. Amy wasn't sure yet whether or not they would be bringing the twins home to Paul's house, or if they would have their own place by then. Alex was optimistic and he had encouraged her to start looking at places. She found a townhouse rental in Mundelein. It was farther from the city, and the schools were good, not that they'd still be renting when the twins were school age. But, maybe they would remain in that area, if they liked it.

Alex and Paul had been busy and in talks with three potential new clients. They were on their way to meet with one of them now. Amy said a prayer for them.

She thought back to the day of her surprise baby shower. Alex had taken her to the salon for some pampering. When they returned, she was surprised to find the house filled with a crowd of friendly faces in a tasteful scene of red and aqua, her two favorite colors. Nick and Jess had generously gifted them the travel system she had registered for. The car seats were black and gray, with the slightest red accents, neutral like Alex wanted and perfect for a boy or girl. She was floored by the outpouring of gifts. They now had everything they needed. She finally felt at ease.

Amy was getting up to go to the bathroom for what seemed like the one hundredth time that day when she heard a pop and felt a gush of warmth flood her pants. *Her water had just broken!* She wasn't sure what to do first. Nobody was home to call for help. She waddled to the toilet and took off soiled undergarments. After peeing she grabbed a pad and put it inside a new pair of panties, to catch any more fluid that might leak out. She was 34 ½ weeks pregnant. The babies would be early, but they weren't too far off, for twins. Her Dr. said she wanted Amy to get to 36 weeks, ideally.

Alex! But he's in an important meeting!? Amy decided not to contact him just yet. She threw a towel over the wet spot in the carpet so they would know where to clean later. She had to get to the hospital. Thankfully there were no contractions yet. Her hospital bag was packed; she had gotten Sharon to help her with that before she had to go back home. The first contraction hit her when she leaned down to grab her bag.

"Ooooaaahh…" she moaned. She tried calling Tina. Jess. Her friend Audrey. Nobody picked up. Another contraction came. She dialed for an ambulance and sent a text to Paul. *My water broke! On way 2 hosp. Tell Alex when ur meetin over pls!*

Chapter 20

Paul

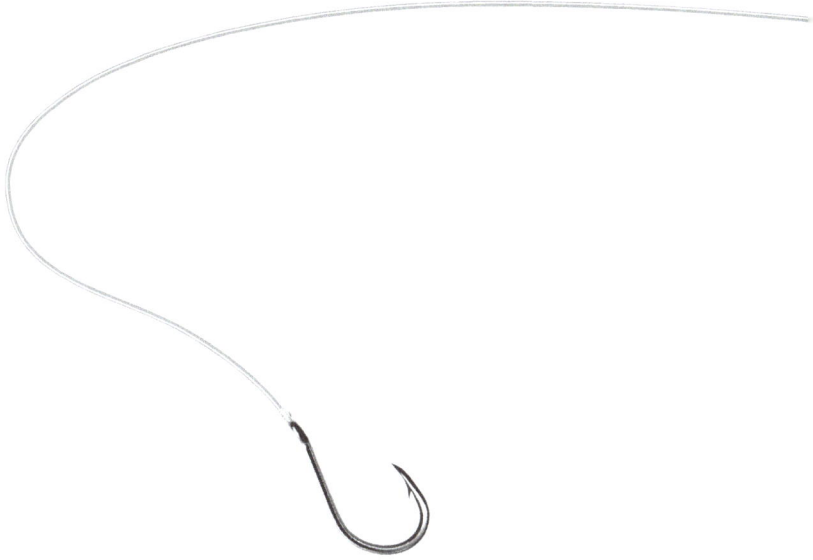

Paul looked over at Alex as they walked up to the meeting. He was glad to see he appeared calm. They had been talking with Derek Steingarton for the last several weeks, and it seemed like he was about ready to sign up, but there was so much riding on their success with this new marketing push, Paul couldn't help but feel nervous. He took a deep breath and let it out slowly to steady himself. *Why did he feel sick? Focus. Alex will do most of the talking anyway.*

But it was just as Jess had said. *"When they're close to making a decision they will want good, solid information about you."*

First, Derek told them he wanted to increase the job. Paul could feel his excitement and anxiety building as he listened to Derek tell them he was looking to expand the scope to multiple branches of his company.

"I'm looking at starting the first year with this branch and by the second year I'd like to be ready to expand these changes to our plants in St. Louis and Philadelphia." Derek looked down at the proposal he was holding. "I like what I see from you guys so far; I'm definitely interested."

"But I won't lie, you're inexperience is a concern. Can you tell me more about yourselves?" He asked.

Paul blurted out something about how he had been working in the industry for the last 9 years, and he had partnered with Alex, who's background was in sales, last March.

"So, you're a startup?" Derek asked. "Okay, I didn't realize that!"

"Is that a deal breaker for you?" Alex questioned.

Derek shook his head. "I suppose under the circumstances, no. You guys definitely seem to know what you're doing. I like the guarantees you offer."

Thank you Jess! Paul thought. Just then his phone buzzed. He looked down to see the text from Amy. *She's in labor.*

Derek sat back in his chair and put his arms behind his head. "So, Paul, you'd be our primary consultant, but I know you're going to be busy with other jobs as well. Would I be able to get a dedicated account manager for our firm?"

Paul tried to keep his composure. He cleared his throat. "I'm sorry, yes. I don't see why that would be a problem." *Should he tell Alex? The meeting was going well. She had said to wait.*

The rest of the meeting was a blur to Paul as Alex calmly negotiated and went over the contract with Derek. A short time later they were leaving the office with a retainer check in hand.

"What's with you, man?" Alex grinned. "We got it! I thought you'd be jumping up and down."

Paul smiled and took the check from Alex, "I'll take this to the bank. You, get your butt to the hospital, Amy's in labor! You know how hard it was for me to keep quiet so we could close this deal?"

"Wait. What? Is she okay?" Alex started to his car then turned back. "She texted you?"

"Yes! She didn't want you distracted from the meeting." Paul said.

"Now go! Your wife needs you, your kids are coming!"

Chapter 21

Alex

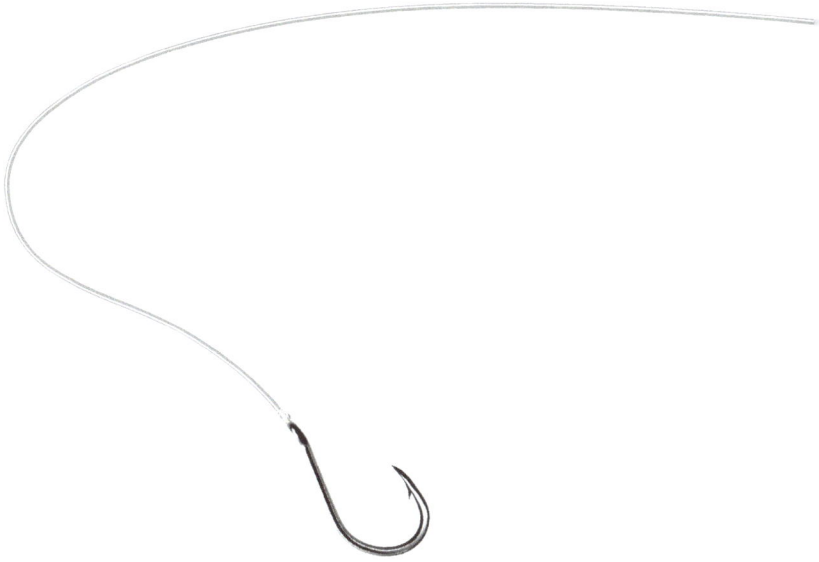

Alex raced through traffic. Everyone was in his way. Amy was all he could think about. *Was she alright? Was she in pain?* He could hardly park. He was so nervous. He ran into the hospital and was breathless as he spoke to the receptionist. "My wife, Amy Murphy is in labor. Where is she?"

"Are you Alex?"

"Yes. Where's my wife?" He was impatient.

"She's expecting you. Room 349."

The elevator was agonizingly slow. He tapped the button for the elevator three more times, as if it would make it come faster. He looked around for the stairs. Finally the doors to the elevator opened.

A moment later he had found Room 349. He rushed in without stopping to knock. He let out a deep breath, relieved to see that everything was alright. She looked beautiful.

He pulled her into his arms and started to cry. "We got it babe. We got the contract!" He stepped back and looked into her eyes. "How are you? What happened?"

Amy smiled at him. "My water broke, that sent me into labor. They gave me antibiotics and a shot of medicine for the babies' lungs. They've been trying to slow my labor but I'm progressing fast. They are getting ready to take me to surgery."

"The babies are coming today?" Alex asked, his face still in tears.

Amy cried too. "Yes, they're coming."

"What can I do?" Alex looked around.

Amy braced herself as another contraction hit. She groaned. After it passed she looked up at Alex. "Stay close and hold my hand."

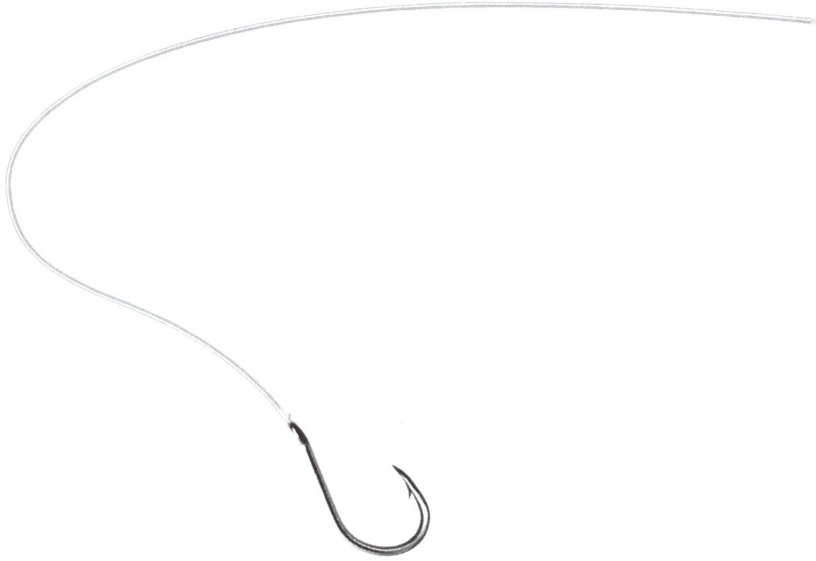

Chapter 22
Amy

Amy felt exhausted and sore, but so happy and content. The surgery had gone well; they had two perfect little girls. She reached in the warmer to touch Baby A's little hand.

"They're beautiful." Alex looked at Amy and smiled. "You did good." He was standing next to Baby B and playing with her foot.

"What are we gonna call them?" Amy asked.

She looked over to Alex. "What do you think of Lydia and Rebekah?"

"Lydia Grace and Rebekah Anne?" Alex suggested, as he pointed to the girls.

Amy laughed and looked down at Lydia. She smiled and said, "Perfect."

Chapter 23
Alex

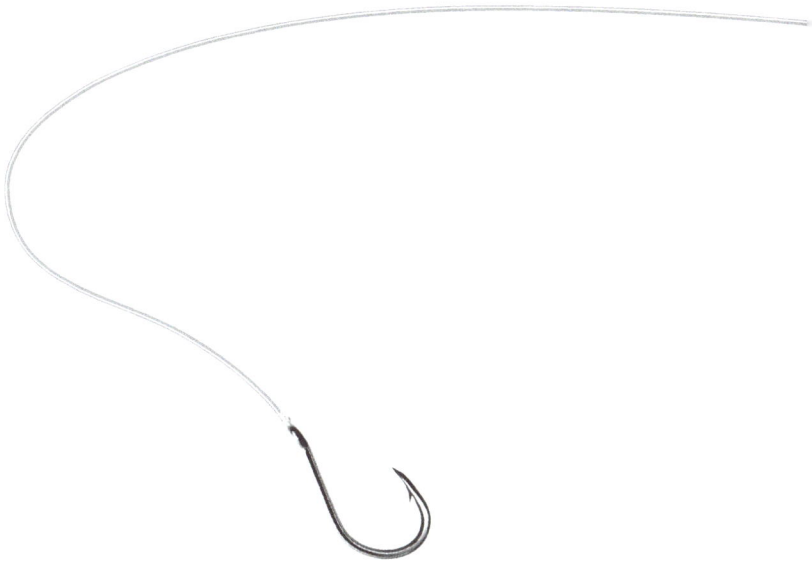

Alex had been scrambling the last 2 weeks. Thankfully the townhouse Amy had her eye on was still available. He had signed a lease and made arrangements with Paul and some other friends to move their stuff over today. This was all a surprise to Amy. She had been released from the hospital 9 days ago but the girls were still in the nursery so she had been spending all her time at the hospital. The hospital had provided a room for her to stay in, without nursing care, since she no longer needed it, so she could remain close to the girls. She had been pumping and working on establishing breastfeeding. Alex admired her resolve. She had been struggling but she hadn't given up. They were all doing well and supposed to come home tomorrow.

With the group of five guys they had, it didn't take more than 4 hours to move everything from the storage unit to the townhouse in Mundelein. Alex and Paul were working on loading the last of their belongings out of Paul's house. They were talking about the new contracts they had just gotten.

"You know, we may have to hire two people! Those ads we're running are pulling more leads for us." Alex said to Paul.

"Remind me to thank Jess for her help again would ya?" Paul laughed as he lifted another box into the back of the truck. "How many are we up to now?"

Alex put the last box in and closed the back door of the truck. "Ninety-seven leads as of this morning." He held up his hand to give Paul a high five.

"Looks like you'll not only get to manage people, you get to figure out how to find them and hire them as well! All the things you wanted." Paul smiled as he climbed into the front seat of the truck. "Don't worry, I got your back."

"Thanks, man. I truly appreciate everything you did to make this work. Without your sister's help I doubt we would have made it." Alex admitted. "We still have to figure out what to get them for their engagement gift."

They were quiet on the drive, both lost in thought. Alex was thinking back on everything that had happened the last several months. Choosing to be an entrepreneur was the hardest and most rewarding thing he had ever done, hands down. As they pulled up to the townhouse he couldn't help but picture how Amy's face will look when he brings Amy and the girls home tomorrow.

Part 2

The Method

As we've seen, the website problems Alex and Paul encountered stemmed from business problems. Each time they had opportunity they ran into the same problems, the same frustrations. When customers came to their site, they couldn't get them to stay. When they finally got a lead, customers were defensive.

With no visible advantage, they were forced to make deep concessions just to win a sale. Customers abused them and they struggled to turn a profit. Their customers didn't respect them. They didn't believe the things they offered were valuable.

All because of the business problems they faced.

As we head into part two, we'll shift gears to discuss the details. What people are drawn to, how to get and keep their attention, how to deal with the (inevitable) resistance that follows attraction, and more.

We'll move fast and dig deep. Are you ready?

Lets go.

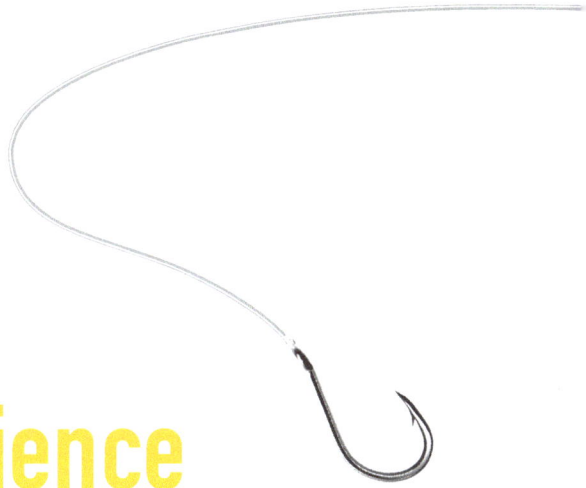

Target Audience

Why the customer you choose controls the amount you'll make

Alan was the worst client ever.
He was combative. He took five weeks to make a decision.
He changed his mind constantly. Figuring out what he wanted was a struggle. He was difficult and he never paid on time.

Alex and Paul hated working with him. But they struggled to attract clients and when they did they were difficult, like Alan. They needed a target audience. They needed to know how to attract the customers they wanted.

But they already had a target audience, or so they thought

Alex knew it was important to choose a target audience. So he chose small business owners. He studied his audience until he knew the demographics and psychographics of his ideal audience by heart. But the ideal audience he chose was broad. If you owned a small business, had money and were willing to pay, you were a 'good fit'.

There's an inherent problem with relying solely on your target audience

Samples.

Take a sample of 3 young men. They're all part of the same scene. They're in their early twenties; all of them are into BMX sports. The three of them wear BMX and skate clothing, and all three of them are shopping for a pair of pants.

It's these similarities that create a target audience right?

Here's the problem.

The first man is 6 ft 4 in tall and he weighs 160 lbs.
The second man is 5 ft 5 in and he's 155 lbs.
The third is 5 ft 9 in and he weighs 175 lbs.

If you're a clothing retailer this seems pretty straight forward. Sell a pair of pants to all three of them, problem solved.

Until you find that they're not *really* shopping for pants

They're looking for a solution. But we need to understand and define the problem first before we know which solution to offer. One man wants a pair of olive green Dickies work pants. Another wants Volcom brand skinny jeans while the third just wants to find a pair of pants that's actually in his size.

Can't you sell to all three at the same time?

Not a chance. Because any angle, any problem you focus on repels the others. Focus on selling Volcom skinny jeans and you lose shoppers searching for olive green Dickies. Focus on big and tall and you lose the others. As we've seen, each of them have very different buying criteria. And they'll use that criteria to filter through their options.

So what do you do?

You focus on a single person. You use that person as your target profile, as the basis for your marketing.
"But focusing on a single person sounds crazy. Can that actually work? Will it work for my business? Can this approach actually bring in more customers?"

Let's look at Manpacks to find out.

It's 2009. Ken Johnson and Andrew Draper suddenly realized that all of their socks had lots of holes in them. "I always need socks, but I never make time to go buy them. Why don't they just show up at my doorstep?" And just like that, Manpacks - manly goods on a schedule - was born.

> "We identified a basic need — we always need socks and underwear — and asked ourselves the question: 'would this work as a subscription?' It just sounded like a funny idea, and we were laughing as we put together the first version of the website." [1]

Aren't there other stores that sell socks, shirts, underwear and razors?

Of course there are, millions of them in fact. But the Walmarts, JCPenneys and Kohl's of the world stopped mattering when they created a profile based on a single person; the busy web pro.

> "The early market we wanted to sell to were web designers and developers, so we hoped this familiarity would appeal to them. It worked far better than we had hoped. By late April we had outsourced our fulfillment operations..."

Fast forward to today and Manpacks has more than 10,000 monthly subscribers. They also managed to raise $500,000 via angel investors. Not too shabby.

Can't you get the same results with personas?

A persona is basically an imaginary friend designed to represent an entire target demographic. You imagine what your 'friend' might say, the attitudes they'd have and how they'd behave.

Here's how Alex created a persona. Using research and his imagination, he filled in the details of his persona's life. He named his persona Seth. Seth was an executive at a large company. He had eight years of experience, he loved to jog and he knew what his 'business' needed.

But there's a problem.

Seth wasn't real.

That meant Seth gave what he had, dummy words and fake emotions. Thing is, Alex knew Seth wasn't real. But he used Seth's dummy words and fake emotions to sell to real people. But real people couldn't relate to his imaginary friend so they refused to buy.

What do dummy words and fake emotions look like?

They're well-meaning but insincere. They're out of touch with the people they're targeting.

Say you're looking for an apartment and you see this:

What does that even mean?

When real people share their stories they talk about their experiences. There's drama, pain and emotion. Take this legendary Zappos marketing story for example:

> "When I came home this last time, I had an email from Zappos asking about the shoes, since they hadn't received them. I was just back and not ready to deal with that, so I replied that my mom had died but that I'd send the shoes as soon as I could. They emailed back that they had arranged with UPS to pick up the shoes, so I wouldn't have to take the time to do it myself. I was so touched. That's going against corporate policy.
>
> Yesterday, when I came home from town, a florist delivery man was just leaving. It was a beautiful arrangement in a basket with white lilies and roses and carnations. Big and lush and fragrant. I opened the card, and it was from Zappos. I burst into tears. I'm a sucker for kindness, and if that isn't one of the nicest things I've ever had happen to me, I don't know what is." [2]

See the difference? There's a realness, an emotional quality to the Zappos story. You felt something.

If you want drama and emotion in a persona, you'll have to make it up. It's not based in reality. That creates a big marketing problem for you because the drama, emotion and words are what all of us are drawn to. But you can only get that from real people.

Which creates another problem, namely that we all feel different things.

Some of us will read the Zappos story and we'll get teary eyed. Others are energized and excited. Some of us won't feel anything. Then there's the skeptics and naysayers who'll disbelieve.

How can you speak to an audience that's filled with so many different people?

You can't, trying to speak to everyone waters down your message. At that point it's unappealing to pretty much everyone. On the other hand if your target profile is Maggie, she has a specific set of problems, emotions and words. Focus on her and suddenly all the 'Maggies' of the world are drawn to your message.[3]

Which means all of them can relate to and empathize with what you're saying.

Your offer acts as an attractor. When your message resonates with them it increases the likelihood that everyone will get what they want.

Once that happens, it's easier to become an 'expert' and to earn their trust. Why? You've focused on a single person and the specific problem they have - the one you can fix.

Focus on one person and suddenly you have a specific audience of people asking -no, demanding- your help. They're eager and happy to spend whatever they need to spend to get your help. And the best part? None of them are like Alan.

Summary

Why focusing on one person is so important

- *"People with money"* isn't a target audience. It's impossible to focus on lots of different people in a target audience.

- Personas rely on guesswork, with no idea if your guess is right.

- A target profile is based on a real person.

- A target profile gives you feedback and lots of meaningful information.

- Building your message around a single person means you attract lots of people that are just like them.

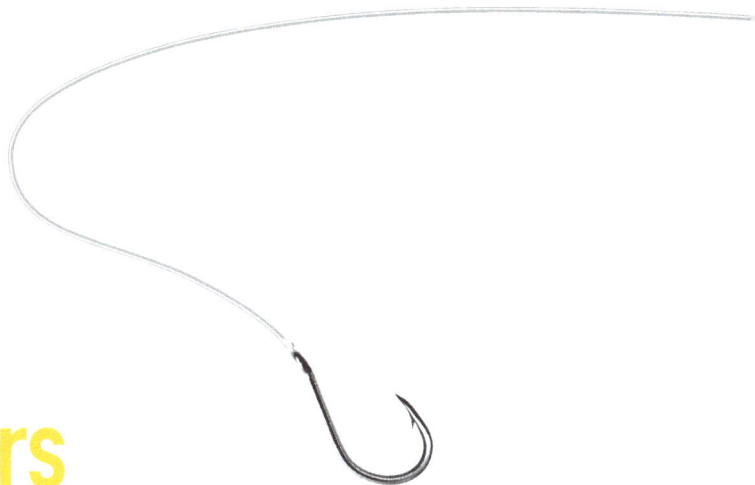

Triggers

You'll never get their attention if you can't fascinate them

You always fall for those.
Just ignore them. Don't look, don't look
Just walk away. Keep walking.

Amy's in the grocery store.
She's waiting in the checkout line.
A quick glance to her left and what does she see?

Gossip magazines.

Now if you're like Amy, your curiosity sucks you right in. In a few short seconds you're knee deep in emotional dysfunction. *Why am I looking at this* you ask yourself as your eyes scan the latest issue. *I came here for milk and eggs, not celebrity divorce drama.*

So why don't you look away?

Because they've used triggers to suck you in to their drama

See, gossip magazines know they're not essential. They know they're an impulse buy. They know they'll have to speak to your emotions if they want your attention. Which leads to the question.

What's a trigger?

Triggers are personality cues that attract attention and create fascination, generating powerful reactions. These cues are the secret ingredients that make any person, business, subject, or topic fascinating. They're the reasons for attraction and they're the reasons behind the things we pay attention to. They're universal and they work on all of us.

Sally Hogshead discovered there are 7 triggers to fascination.[1]

POWER displays command over circumstances, people and self. It's the confident, opinionated Tomboy you grew up with. It's Suze Orman on CNBC and Leonidas from the movie 300.

PASSION is sensory, intuitive, expressive and feeling. Passionate people tend to be the life of the party. The salesman that befriends everyone, the social butterfly that bonds with people in any group and those that wear their hearts on their sleeves.

MYSTIQUE, at its core, is curiosity. It entices with unanswered questions, puzzles and unfamiliarity. It's those mysterious new internet acronyms everyone's using, Google's search algorithms and Coca-Cola's secret formula. It's the mysterious 'bad boy' women are so attracted to and the cute yet shy librarian that knows what antepenultimate[2] means.

PRESTIGE uses symbols of hierarchy, rank and achievement to earn respect. The luxury cars that signal affluence and create jealousy. It's the coveted backstage pass and wining an Academy Award. It's being at the top, part of the elite.

ALARM screams consequences, danger and loss. It's the screeching tires that create intense focus and fear, the bad news at work, and impending danger. It's the Hells Angel parked next to you and the dog poop you're about to step in.

REBELLION is the forbidden fruit. It's the defiant drive that pushes us outside of what's acceptable, into the realm of taboo. The I-want-what-I-can't-have-you're-not-the-boss-of-me mindset. It's eating at the Heart Attack Grill[3] and ignoring your mom when she tells you to stay out of the cookie jar.

TRUST craves certainty, predictability and reliability. It's the predictable reliability of routine, the comfort of knowing what to expect, and the building blocks of loyalty in our relationships. It's knowing that your UPS package will arrive on time and the confidence that a coke will taste like a coke.

These triggers are the building blocks to everything we find fascinating.

Now you might be wondering, how do I use these triggers?

You'll want to start by identifying the cues that are built-in to your product or service. Selling insurance? You're actually selling protection. Lean on TRUST and ALARM. Luxury condos? Lead with POWER and PRESTIGE. Selling a not-so healthy product? Embrace and flaunt taboos to create REBELLION. Need to sell with a secret formula or algorithm that you don't want to give away? Grab their interest with MYSTIQUE.

What if you don't know what makes your product, service or business fascinating? What if it's not built-in?

What if you've created something that mainstream consumers have never seen before? Like the first portable mp3 player?

In 1998, Korea's Saehan Information Systems launched the very first Mp3 player. The MPMan F10.

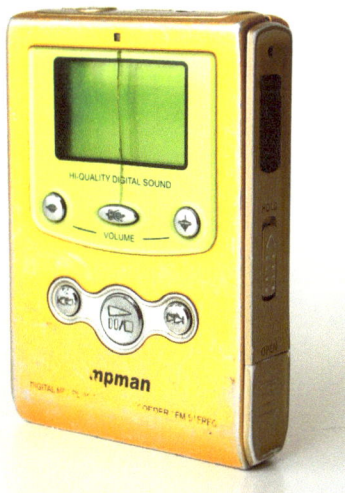

It was innovative, but critics and consumers hated it.

The next year Diamond released the Rio PMP300. They added new features with the goal of improving on the MPMan design. The Mp3 player wasn't mainstream yet, but consumer interest had started to grow. Diamond would ship more than 200,000 units.

Then along came the iPod.

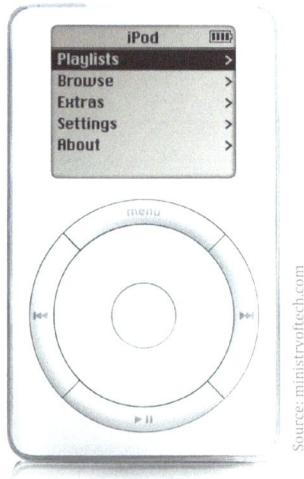

Source: ministryoftech.com

Steve Jobs and his team at Apple seized the moment, launching the iPod in 2001. But in the beginning there were problems. Mac-only availability and high prices meant sales were slow at first. For the first three to four years Apple worked on addressing the problems.

Then came the silhouettes.

Suddenly, our culture was obsessed with the iPod. Time magazine hailed the iPod as something that launched the Apple renaissance, and completely redefined the experience of listening to music.[4] The iPod, along with the white earbuds, had become a cultural revolution--everybody wanted one.

But a cultural revolution requires fascination. What was so fascinating about the iPod?

PASSION, PRESTIGE, MYSTIQUE and REBELLION came together to create the perfect storm. While there were a number of factors that made the iPod a cultural icon, our attraction and fascination began with their message.

The iPod is cool.

If you want to fit in, if you're hot, you have an iPod.

The silhouette campaign told us that iPod customers were cool, passionate and free. The faceless people dancing in the ads created mystique and allowed us to project our subconscious desire for acceptance, popularity, and status on to them.

Celebrity silhouettes amplified our desire for PRESTIGE. Using the same mp3 players as our favorite musicians meant we were part of a special club.

And so a cultural icon was born.

But there's a problem. You're not a cultural icon and you're not Apple.

So how do you know if your message is fascinating?

The six symptoms of fascination are simple. These six points help you evaluate how attractive your message (or company) is. The more you answer yes to, the more fascinating you are.

1. You create strong or intense emotional reactions.

2. What you do sparks discussion or intense debate.

3. You create customer evangelists.

4. Competitors rearrange their strategy or business around you.

5. You spark a social revolution.

6. You're "cultural shorthand" for a set of values or actions.

1. You create strong or intense emotional reactions.

What happens when you create an experience people love so much they choose to ignore their bodily functions?

Apple knows.

If you've been in an Apple store, you know they use black balls as seating in their stores. What you may not know is that those balls are affectionately referred to as "pee balls". Apparently, when kids are really into a game they will often choose to just pee their pants so they don't have to move. The result? Spongey pee-soaked seats. [5]

A seat with the black cover removed. See the pee stains?

Source: http://www.reddit.com/r/apple/comments/19r9px/dont_ever_sit_on_the_black_balls_at_the_kids/

True, all of this could simply be an unfortunate coincidence; except for the fact that this isn't happening in Walmart, Best Buy or Target. Apple fans are so enthralled with their products they're willing to risk shame, embarrassment and awkward social encounters so they can spend more time with their products. Strong, intense emotion for sure. But are we as adults immune? Not so much.

In fact, millions of adults will spend hours waiting in line for the newest iPhone, Playstation or Xbox. Devoted fanboys will wait for the newest movie blockbuster in full costume. Tens of thousands of people plaster the name "Harley Davidson" on their bodies in the form of tattoos. In each of these examples there's an intense emotional reaction taking place.

2. What you do sparks discussion or intense debate.

Microsoft vs. Apple. Pepsi vs. Coke. Star Wars vs. Star Trek. Smith & Wesson vs. Ruger. Batman vs. Iron man. What do these rivalries have in common? Intense debate. In each of these examples there are millions of loyal fans and skeptics fighting, arguing and endlessly debating about which one is better.

It's all subjective of course, but that's not the point. These brands have snagged our attention. As a result, we're ready to take on all comers. Insult Steve Jobs and watch as Apple fanboys come pouring out of the woodwork to defend his reputation.

3. You create customer evangelists.

And what are fanboys if not evangelists? Evangelists can be paid but the best ones work for free. They promote your products. They act as your informal sales force, spreading your gospel to the unconverted. They support your business voluntarily and they'll fight for the chance to spend more of their money on your products.[6]

4. Competitors rearrange their strategy or business around you.

The iPod's white earbuds became a status symbol so much so that for a while, it was uncool to use anything else. Competitors scrambled to copy the iPod's earbud design and they began to mass produce their low priced knockoffs.

Suddenly competitors were absorbing and copying Apple's designs.[7] They took their innovations and used them to create cheaper knockoffs. Instead of finding their uniqueness, competitors became content to simply follow.

5. You spark a social revolution.

People that didn't have an iPod started buying knockoff mp3 players with white earbuds in an effort to pass as an Apple user. Ten years later and competitors are still copying the iconic "white earbuds". But their impact didn't stop there. With iTunes, they forever changed the way we buy our music.

In the past, radio DJs and billboard charts told us which albums were "hot". If your favorite band released new tracks you went out and bought the album. iTunes replaced Radio DJs. Suddenly "hot" was whatever songs you had on repeat. You no longer needed to buy the entire album to gain access to your favorite songs.

6. You've become "cultural shorthand" for a set of values or actions.

The Twitter hashtag consists of a word or phrase that's prefixed with the hashsign (#). It was originally a new way for users to organize and find tweets on Twitter. Usage quickly evolved and users began to use them to tag objects, express emotions or share feelings.

When the Anthony Weiner sexting scandal broke,[8] Twitter users found tweets pointing to the story by searching with the hashtag #Weinergate.

Weiner was busted for showing his... you know.

Source: http://sindywarren.com/weinergate-you-cant-make-this-s-up-and-what-hr-can-learn-from-it/

But hashtags have gone beyond Twitter, appearing in emails, text and instant messages, and even in-person conversations.

And when Chris Messina, a Google developer advocate wanted to introduce two of his friends to each other via email, he added a quick #Introduction in his subject line. No need, he explained, for a long preamble when a quick, to-the-point hashtag would do.[9]

The hashtag became a sort of cultural shorthand that was used to add humor, meaning and context to conversations - both online and offline.

By now you should have a pretty good idea about whether your organization is fascinating or not.

If you answered yes to at least one of the above statements you're on your way. With a little guidance and a lot of work, you can become an attraction powerhouse.

What if your answer was no on all counts? If you've evaluated your fascination levels and found they're not where you'd like them to be don't worry, there's plenty of time to turn things around. And it starts with identifying the factors that influence which triggers you use.

The factors that influence which triggers you use:

1. The problems built into your business, product or service.

2. Customer fears and expectations.

3. Your personal triggers.

4. Your competitor's triggers.

5. The customer response you're looking for.

1. The problems built into your business, product or service.

Each industry comes with risk factors and objections. Each of these objections is an opportunity to create fascination. Here's an example.

Liberty Mutual
If you own a car you're familiar with the basics of car insurance coverage. If we buy a new car and it's totaled, our insurance company gives us the value of what our car is worth at that point in time.

Most of the time that means we're going to get less than we've paid. Liberty Mutual relieves customer fears with their New Car Replacement Guarantee. If your car is totaled in the first year they'll give you the money for a brand new car, not just the depreciated value. They include that as a standard feature with every new policy.[10]

They've taken a systemic problem affecting the entire industry and they've turned it into a TRUST factor. Now customers feel comfortable and at ease with them instead of bracing for a fight with their claims adjuster. Every totaled car they replace builds on the trustworthy reputation they've worked so hard to create.

2. Customer fears and expectations.

In 1973, Dominos Pizza created their famous guarantee, 30 minutes or it's free. Their guarantee was a win/win for customers and it became well known.
Then came the accidents.

In 1992, Dominos settled a lawsuit filed by the family of an Indiana woman who was killed by a Domino's delivery driver, paying the family $2.8 million.

In 1993 a Dominos pizza delivery driver ran a red light and slammed into Jean Kinder. She sued and won a $15 million dollar settlement.

Rumors began to spread that Dominos delivery drivers were running children down while delivering pizzas. Dominos developed a reputation for "reckless driving and irresponsibility" according to former CEO Tom Monaghan. Dominos was faced with some pretty bad fallout. They needed to rebuild TRUST to deal with the fallout.

This whole ordeal created ALARM. And what does ALARM do? It draws our attention to problems. Problems we want fixed. Defuse the problem, restore consistency and routine, and in time, you'll rebuild TRUST.

3. Your personal triggers.

My personal trigger would be MYSTIQUE and POWER. That says certain things about me. I'm careful, methodical and deliberate. I like having a plan. Awesome right? Except this means I'm less likely to use PASSION.

And that means I'm comfortable doing things a certain way.

This means you'll need to have a pretty good idea of where you're at and what you're willing to do. Naturally this creates some limitations. Unsure about your personal fascination triggers? Visit Sally's site for more information on your F-Score.

4. Your competitor's triggers.

What if Bill Gates started dressing like Steve Jobs? What if he started wearing the same turtlenecks and jeans? What would happen to him? To Microsoft?

Apple fanboys would be outraged. Gates would be laughed at, he'd be criticized, his inbox would fill with hate mail. He'd never live it down.

When you copy a competitor, you're not fascinating. It's been done before. This means you'll need to have a clear idea of who your competitors are and the triggers they're using if you want to attract customers.

5. The customer response you're looking for.

Apple tied PRESTIGE and PASSON to the iPod. Coca-Cola tied MYSTIQUE to their formula. The Heart Attack Grill tied REBELLION and ALARM to their brand.[11] These businesses understand that the triggers you use dictate not only the response you'll get, but who you'll attract.

"So the triggers we use control who we attract and how they respond. Where in my business can I use these triggers?"

Use these triggers in your...

Purpose: Why your organization exists.

Ethos: Your morals, values and principles. What you believe and what you stand for.

Culture: This encompasses the attitude, culture, identity and personality of your organization.

History: Your beginnings, history and back-story.

Offers: The products, services and information you create.

Promises: The benefits, expectations and rewards you promise.

Behavior: How you conduct business, how you treat others.

Using these triggers attracts customers, creates fans and encourages buy-in. There's a catch though. Once customers buy-in to your business it stops being yours. That's because with a feeling of ownership comes a belief that they have a say in how you do business.

So what does it look like when fans "buy-in" to your business?

When Coca-Cola decided to change their secret formula in 1983, their fans were furious. Most customers accepted the new formula but Coke fans were more vocal. Coca-Cola had changed their product, the product they had bought into. There was hell to pay. Coca-Cola received 1,500 calls per day and more than 400,000 angry calls and letters.

One letter, delivered to then CEO Roberto Goizueta, was addressed to "Chief Dodo, The Coca-Cola Company". Another letter wanted the autograph of "one of the dumbest executives in American business history" on the premise it would later become valuable.

So they were upset. How do we know that fans had bought into the Coca-Cola culture? A psychiatrist Coke hired to listen in on calls told Coca-Cola execs that some people sounded as if they were discussing the death of a family member. Using triggers in these areas enabled Coca-Cola to attract likeminded people - people that shared the same values and had a bond with their product.

Sharing the same values, creating a bond? Being fascinating sounds a lot like manipulation.

And the reason it can feel sleazy is due to the fact that you now have inside knowledge. That makes you powerful. You're able speak to people in a way that bypasses their natural resistance. You're able to get to the heart of what attracts them. Persuasion is suddenly easier.

Using the knowledge you have to control others is sleazy and wrong. But it's not manipulative if it's used honestly. Imagine that you're about to step in dog poo. I see that you're about to make a stinky mistake and yell "poo, look out!" [ALARM]. You catch yourself and walk around safely.

You're relieved. But that wasn't manipulative. Why? *Because the threat you faced was real.* Did I use these triggers to control you or was I simply stating the obvious?

I stated the obvious.

If I manipulate your emotions selfishly or I deceived you when you expected me to tell you the truth then I've done something wrong.

And that's the position that most customers are in. Most of the time they come with an understanding of their problem, but often times it's hazy. Customers tend to have an incomplete knowledge of the issues they face. But you're the expert and you can see the trouble ahead. So you tell them. You use your triggers to cut through their filters, show them the problem and present the solution.

Do you really need triggers to tell them about their problems? There are plenty of blogs, websites, and ads that do just fine without them.

It's certainly possible to communicate without triggers. The problem is that your message has to make it through their filters before they can act on it. Filters like *"I'm busy right now, I'll read that later"* or *"can you email it?"* We both know what happens to messages like these.

But aren't we using triggers automatically already? Why do we need to learn about "fascination" if that's the case?

Because we're inconsistent. And our inconsistency comes from a lack of knowledge. So we attract people in spurts. Sometimes we're lucky, but most of the time we're not. That makes it hard to attract attention and harder to get people to listen to what you have to say.

Triggers are the key to attraction and persuasion. Gossip magazines understand that their message needs to make it past your filters if they stand a chance. It's no different for you. Speak to their emotions if you want their attention.

Summary

Why you need triggers if you want attention

- These seven triggers or personality cues form the basis of attraction and persuasion.

- These personality cues are universal. They're part of who we are.

- We use triggers everyday whether we know about them or not.

- Certain factors and situations determine which triggers should be used.

- You can use triggers in your message, your offers, history, behavior and a number of other places.

- If you're not in the know, you use triggers accidentally and in spurts. It's tough to be consistent if you're not sure how the formula works.

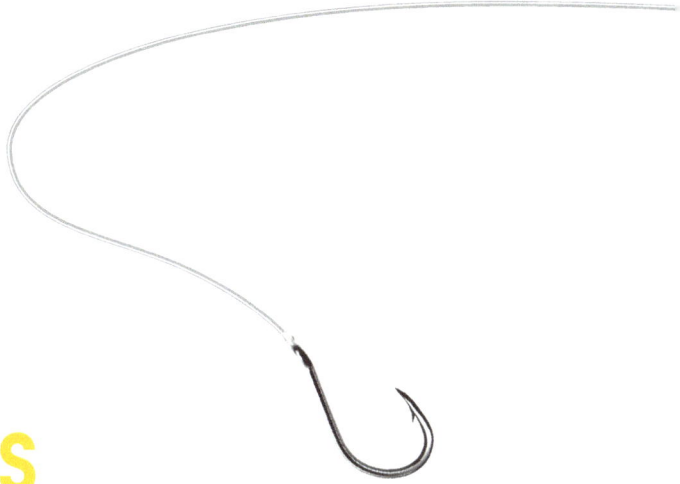

Problems

Why we need them, why we're drawn to them

Alex weaved through traffic. Amy was in labor.
He was agitated. *Get out of my way!*
As he sped down the highway and zipped through traffic, all he could think about was Amy.

He wasn't paying attention to his surroundings. He wasn't even aware of the fact that he was 15 miles over the speed limit.

Until he saw the flashing lights.

All at once, he panicked and pumped the brakes. "Getting pulled over is NOT what I need right now," he fumed. And in that moment, he wasn't thinking about Amy or his babies. He wasn't even thinking about getting to the hospital.

He was thinking about one thing. Not getting a ticket.

And while getting pulled over and receiving a ticket is unpleasant, it certainly doesn't trump the birth of your child. So what caused his momentary shift in focus?

His negative bias.

But he's not the only one. All of us have these negative biases.

See, each of us is born with what researchers call a "negative bias".[1] Dr. John Cacioppo at the University of Chicago discovered that our brains react more strongly to stimuli it thinks is negative. He showed people pictures that would trigger positive feelings (pizza or a Ferrari), pictures that would stir up negative feelings (a mutilated face or dead cat) and pictures that would trigger neutral feelings (a plate, a hair dryer). He recorded activity in the brain and discovered there's a greater surge in brain electrical activity when we view something we think is negative. He also found that our attitudes are heavily influenced by bad news more so than by good news, by problems more than solutions.

Because we're all obsessed with problems.

But this isn't something we learn as we get older. As soon as we're born, we begin an obsessive, never ending quest to find problems.[2, 3] And it's important because doing that keeps us alive, happy and out of harm's way.[4]

Our obsession with problems is at work in every part of our lives, working to keep us safe.

Imagine you're on the highway. You're stuck in traffic with slow moving cars and lots of impatient people. You're not sure what's going on but you're annoyed and curious at the same time. *What's the hold-up?* you wonder.

And then you see it.

You see the police and firefighters. You see the jagged pieces of metal and the shards of glass.

And even though you were annoyed just a few short seconds ago, you do what everyone else does. You slow down and stare at the wreckage. Suddenly your mind is filled with thoughts and questions. What happened? Is everybody okay? Is there anything I can do? [5]

And if there's an opportunity for you to help you'll do it. You'll call for help, you'll work side by side with people you don't know and you'll offer a solution to those that need it.

Which leads us to a fairly simple conclusion.

Our brains need to discover the problem before we're ready for the solution.

In our story, Alex focused on avoiding a ticket *after* he saw the flashing lights. Was he thinking of an excuse before he saw them? Not at all. His focus was getting to the hospital. His police problem created a strong trigger [ALARM] that prompted him to immediately think of a solution.

And because problems are naturally alarming, they create stress and anxiety.

Let's say that you're watching TV during prime time. In the middle of a commercial break your local news anchor comes on and begins with "tonight at 10". What usually comes out of their mouth next? Tragedy. Pain. Sadness. News that's horrifying. News that's shocking.

And in most cases, regardless of whether you watch or not, your curiosity is aroused. You want to learn more. So many of us decide to tune in at ten for more details. If your news anchor mentions there's a serial killer roaming around in your neighborhood, you'll probably want to know that the police are looking for him. You may invest in some form of protection. But the obvious point here is this: you wouldn't be searching for a solution to a problem that doesn't exist.

You may be wondering what this has to do your website and marketing.

Think about the marketing you've seen in the last week. What do most marketers focus their attention on? The solution. The vast majority of marketing leads with solutions, often disguised as "features and benefits" while problems, for the most part, are ignored. If you're in sales or marketing you've probably heard things like: "sell the benefits" or "sell the sizzle not the steak". And so the majority of marketers focus on solutions, ignoring the problem.

But ignoring the problem is a bad idea because most of the time, customers aren't even aware of each and every problem they'll have to deal with.

Does this mean that the solution isn't important?

Not at all. In fact, the solution is just as important as the problem. This makes context, specificity and timing pretty important. Why? Because they show you how to present the problem in a way that attracts customer attention.

Let's take a closer look at each of these factors.

1.   Finding the right problem.

2.   Using a customer's own words.

3.   Timing and context.

1. Finding the right problem.

Every product or service solves many problems. In fact, there's a long list of problems that customers want you to solve. But the problem we want to solve isn't always the main issue customers are focused on. We react strongly to things *we view as problems.* But the problem you focus on may not be that big of a deal for customers.

Take something as simple as drinking water.

- Some people won't buy water if it has fluoride in it

- Others believe that tap water is dirty or unsafe

- Or that bottled water is an unnecessary, environmental hazard

- Then there are those who believe that drinking anything besides distilled water is a bad idea

- The filter fans argue that you're drinking metal and minerals without the right filter

And the list goes on and on. You see the problem? If you're selling water, which one of those is most important to your customer? Which one gets their attention? I'll tell you. It's the main problem, the one that matters most to them.

So how do you go about finding the problem that matters most?

By asking. Which is why the target profile interview is so important. Sitting down with a real person gives you the opportunity to ask them about their problems. They'll rank your problems and tell you which issue is at the top of *their list.*

2. Using a customer's own words.

When you speak to someone about their problem you get a lot of non-verbal communication. The words people choose convey specific emotions and feelings. The words they use and the way they communicate, tells you about their personality.

Do they use a lot of emotional words or are they all about results, numbers and getting down to business? The words they choose tell you a lot about their understanding of the problem, misconceptions they might have and a lot of other useful stuff. But you can't get that "stuff" from a persona.

3. Timing and context.

Problems need timing and context. You'll need to know how to say it, when to say it and how much to say if you want people to do what you're asking.

Dump too many problems on people in your message and they become overwhelmed. They simply freeze. Instead of going for what you're offering (or even a competitor) they do nothing. A straight forward example of this is the dreaded wall of text.

What do we do when we see this? Most of us freeze or ignore the message.

Source: http://blog.ziggytek.com/2011/06/06/apples-retail-anniversary-poster-isa-wall-of-text/

And then there's timing. Share problems at the wrong time and you get the wrong reaction. Upsell at an inappropriate time or fail to discuss a problem when you were supposed to and customers are angry.

Imagine that your car was totaled (everyone's okay). What if your insurance claims adjuster tried to upsell you on his company's new insurance product, before giving you your check. That would be sleazy right?

And what if that same claims adjuster told that they'd pay for the tax, title and insurance when you buy a new car, but neglected to tell you that you'd need to buy one within 30 days? Upsetting no?

This is why context, specificity and timing are so important. While we're obsessed with problems, there's a right way and a wrong way to use them.

Wait a sec. Aren't we just manufacturing problems to scare customers?

Problems are an inherent part of what we do. Often times, solving one problem creates another. Here's an example of what I mean.

On February 10th, 2007 Amazon released the Kindle and sold it for $399 dollars. It sold out in five and a half hours, remaining out of stock for five months. Customers loved everything about it. The fact that you could take notes, highlight and bookmark pages. The fact that the Kindle 1 seemed to eliminate all of the problems inherent to paper books.

Then came the Kindle 2.

It had a smaller, more functional keyboard, you could use it with either hand and the resolution was much better.[6] The Kindle 2 made all the flaws of the original Kindle 1 crystal clear.

This created a problem.

The Kindle 1 was slow. It wasn't as pretty, or as fast. The resolution wasn't as clear. Even worse, the Kindle 2 was cheaper. And that created stress. If you had a Kindle 1 you remember what it was like to look at the Kindle 2. And this concept is replayed in thousands of ways with millions of products.

Today's new solution is tomorrow's problem. We know that manufacturers aren't doing this out of spite. They're doing their very best to solve our problems today with what they have now. Yet solving our problems creates new ones. And so the never ending hunt for problems continues.

And what can we learn from the hunt?

That we're not creating artificial problems to scare customers into buying from us. We're pointing out problems as they exist now. We're drawing their attention to issues that need their attention but may have flown under their radar.

All this talk about problems and our "negative bias" sounds really ...well ...negative.

And while it sounds that way on the surface it's really not. It's equivalent to telling friends and loved ones about the bad food you ate at that new place in town or the online retailer that took your money and disappeared.

James Altucher wrote about how he stopped a 10 million dollar robbery.[7] A guy he calls "M" tried to use his shares in a well known private internet company (worth 25 million) as leverage to borrow 10 million dollars from his friend "Bill".

But the whole thing was a fraud. What would've happened if James decided to ignore the problems he saw and let his friend handle things on his own? What if he wasn't actively participating in the process with Bill? His friend would've lost a lot of money. The loss to his friend would have been catastrophic and deeply humiliating.

Was James being negative? Was he fear mongering? Not at all. He did the right thing. He protected his friend and prevented a robbery, saving him from the hurt and fallout that would definitely have followed.

Which is why we're not being negative when we direct our customer's attention to the problem.

It's true, when we alert customers to problems they weren't aware of, we freak them out. Problems create stress and anxiety. But like the police officer waiting for Alex, the problems your customers will face are already out there, whether they know it or not. Share the problem and you'll save them from a painful and potentially expensive experience.

Summary
Why we need problems

- We're naturally drawn to problems. Finding problems helps us stay safe.

- Problems naturally create alarm, stress and anxiety. We need relief from this kind of stress.

- We aren't ready for a solution until we're aware of (and accept) the problem.

- It's important to find the problem that matters most to your audience.

- Pointing out the problem protects your customer. It's not negative or manipulative if the problem is genuine and the threat is real.

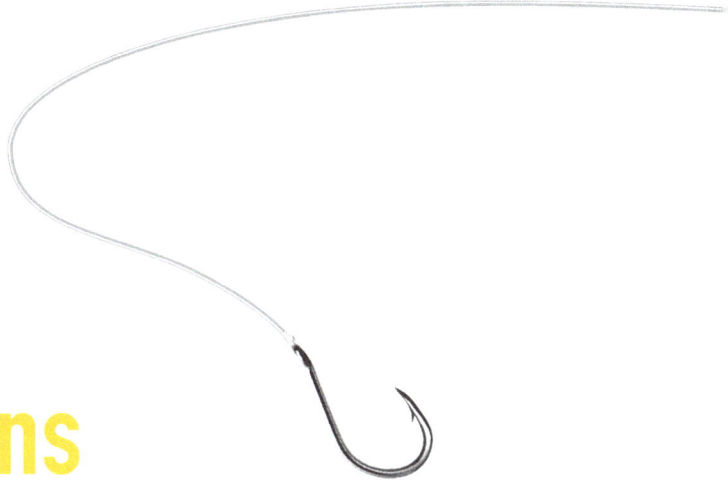

Solutions

Why no one cares when you offer yours

"Please not me, please not me."

Alex watched as the squad car pulled out behind him. As he stared at the flashing lights, he thought about what he'd say to the officer. Almost instantly, a terrifying thought popped into his head.

What if you're not there when the girls are born?

He cringed as he tried to block out that thought. He knew that in a few seconds he'd have to pull over, but once he did that he wouldn't be able to control how long the officer would take.

And then he saw the solution.

Don't stop. You'll get there in time if you just keep going.
What about the cop behind me?
Let them know what's going on.

He dialed 911 and told the dispatcher about his problem. As he glanced to his left he saw that the squad car was suddenly right next to him. The officer signaled for him to follow.

And that's just what the solution does, it follows.

But what does the solution follow? To get the answer, we first need to define what we mean by "solution". Quite simply, a solution answers a specific problem. In Alex's case he didn't want to stop for the police and miss out on the birth of his two daughters, his police escort was the solution.

Because the solution follows the problem.

Earlier I mentioned that the solution is just as important as the problem, yet we're naturally drawn to the problem. Does this mean the solution isn't really that important?

It's actually the opposite. Yes it's true, our brains react more strongly to problems. But that doesn't mean we enjoy it or want the experience to last. Problems are stressful. They show us something needs to be fixed. The solution fixes the problem and relieves our stress. It's used to restore balance and right wrongs.

Problems *create* stress and anxiety.
Solutions *relieve* stress and anxiety.

It's not an either/or proposition because we need both.

A solution can't relieve a non-existent problem.

It can't right a wrong that doesn't exist. Which is why the solution needs to come after the problem. Imagine Alex had plenty of time, he wasn't worried about missing the birth of his girls and he wasn't getting pulled over in the first place.

Would dialing 911 be a solution for him to use? Would he be worried about the police officer pulling him over and taking his sweet time? Of course not. If there's no problem there's no need for a solution, because problems give solutions context.

Customers have lots of problems and they're looking for solutions.

Yet there's never just one solution to a customer's problem is there? There are often hundreds, even thousands of competitors offering a solution to the same problem.

And that's part of the reason why customers aren't responding like they should. If the problem is missing and your solution seems generic, it's easy for customers to tune you out because your offer is just like everyone else's. But stick a problem in front of your solution and suddenly you attract attention.

Let's take a look at a real life example to see how the problem and solution work together.

The FIJI water company bottles water from the islands of Fiji. They felt their water was pristine and much cleaner than tap water from say, Cleveland.[1] After all, tap water's dirty right? Why should the people of Cleveland drink sludge when they can drink water from the pristine rainforests of Fiji! So they created a slogan.

> *"The label says FIJI because it's not bottled in Cleveland".* [2]

Then they decided to launch an ad campaign to share the "good news".

So the Cleveland water department, through no fault of their own, had a problem. Their water was being labeled as dirty. These unflattering ads had painted their city in a negative light, attracting attention for the wrong reasons. The city water department took this campaign as an insult. Residents were asking questions and the city needed a solution.

So the Cleveland water department decided to run some tests. They compared FIJI water to Cleveland water and some other national brands.

These tests found that FIJI water was lower quality, lost in taste tests against Cleveland water, and cost much, much more. FIJI water contained 6.3 micrograms of arsenic per liter, while the city's tap water was arsenic free.

The FIJI water company quietly pulled their ads after test results were released.[3]

See what's happening here?

No one cared about Cleveland water before FIJI's ad campaign. But that campaign created a problem. That problem, created demand for a solution. People needed to know FIJI's claims weren't true. They need to know the city's drinking water was safe and clean.

In each case, the problem attracts attention and the solution holds attention. Until we confuse solution with process.

Because there's a difference between solution and process.

Process is a step-by-step methodology you use to fix the problem, while a solution is simply the answer to that problem.

What would it look like if the Cleveland water department described their process?

> *Water is filtered through precisely graded sand and gravel performing a "natural polishing". Filtered water flows into clear wells for its final chemical application. From finished water reservoirs water flows to the distribution system.*[4]

But we want a solution.

Most of the time we don't care about the process we just want a solution to our problem. When Cleveland residents are thirsty they want clean, contaminant free drinking water. Cleveland's tap water is certified clean.

In our example, the solution mirrors the problem.

Which is exactly how your solution needs to be structured in order to provide relief from the problem. If the problem is contaminated water, the solution is clean water. If migraines are the problem, migraine relief is the solution.

The solution is simply the problem's opposite. It's not clever, there's no hype and no drama. It's there to provide relief.

Summary

How to get customers to care about your solution

- The solution is just as important as the problem. But the solution needs to come after the problem.

- Solutions relieve the stress and anxiety that problems create.

- It's easy to confuse solution with process. Process is a step-by-step methodology while the solution is simply the answer that solves the problem.

- The solution mirrors the problem. If back pain is the problem, back pain relief is the solution.

Objections

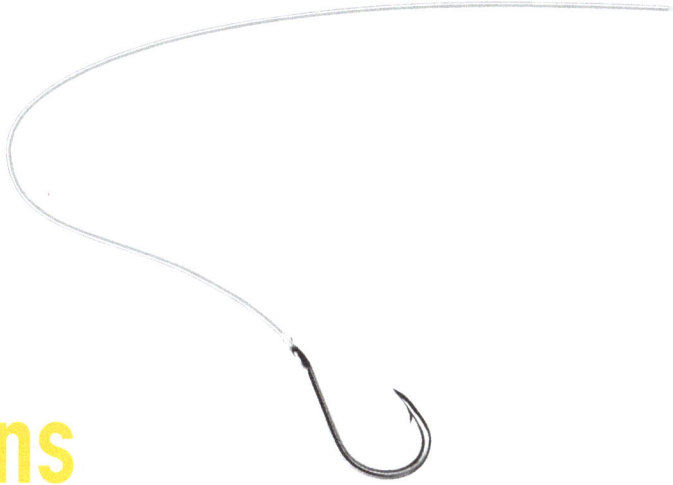

The inevitable part of selling that gets worse if you run

"I'm interested but..."

Whenever Alex and Paul were close to a sale, customer fears kicked in.

Their price was too high.
They weren't experienced enough.
Customers wanted time to think things over.

Naturally, they were afraid of these objections. They felt they couldn't answer them all so they did what they thought made the most sense. They tried to hide them.

Why do customers make objections in the first place?

We all make objections in an effort to protect ourselves. Objections keep us safe. They protect us from making a mistake (and the embarrassment that follows). When we make a decision about anything, we do our best to justify that decision in our heads. Objections are part of the justification process. We want to be sure we're making the right choice.

And as consumers, making the right choice means creating a wall of objections.

But obviously that wall of objections depends on the amount of risk you're taking on right? If you're buying a new car, you're definitely going to have more objections than someone buying a bicycle right?

Actually, no.

We seem to revolve around the same six or seven objections regardless of what we're buying. And while we rephrase and repackage our objections they can all be traced back to three root causes.

1. Past experiences.

These experiences can be ours or someone else's. Burned by a salesman in the past? Dealt with empty warranty promises? Your objections will reflect that. You'll ask more questions and get a second, third and even fourth opinion until you're satisfied. Bad experiences mean you're more likely to leave at the first sign of trouble.

2. Your Perceptions.

Perceptions like "this sales rep is only after my money" or "car salesmen are all dishonest crooks" create resistance. They influence our thoughts and beliefs, shaping the choices we make. Our perceptions tend to be the first cause of objections.

3. A genuine need to know (Inexperience).

There can be a fear of the unknown if you're buying something for the first time. Is this safe? What am I getting myself into? What don't I know? Chances are you'll have doubts based simply on the fact that this experience is unfamiliar. You haven't done this before. Naturally, there's a lot that you need to know.

Does this mean an objection is a No?

Most of the time, it's a request for reassurance. Customers are asking you to address any obstacles in the way before they feel it's safe to continue. We justify a customer's fears and make things worse when we try to hide from the objections. Our stomachs sink when a customer brings up an objection and it's the part of the sales process most of us hate.

The Seven Objections

1. **Price:** Your price is too high, I can get it cheaper, etc.

2. **Complacent:** We're fine right now. Don't need to do anything. I can do it myself.

3. **Distrust:** How do I know you have the experience? Have you done this before? What happens if...?

4. **Insider Politics:** They have someone else in mind and/or they have no intention of actually working with you.

5. **Timing:** Can you call me again in 6 months? I just don't have the money right now. I need time to think about it.

6. **Political:** They already have someone they plan on hiring. They may or may not be using you for leverage.

7. **Disinterest:** Send me some information and I'll look it over. I'll think about it. I'll let you know. I'm not really interested.

And this hatred leads us to believe that objections are the enemy.

But it's actually the opposite. Objections are signals that a customer is interested (at some level) in what you're offering. If they weren't interested they'd simply leave.

When customers bring up objections they're telling you about the reasons they won't buy. They're telling you about the problems that keep them from committing. And they're showing you what you need to do to make the sale.

Here's an example.

A close friend finds a great deal on Groupon for scuba diving lessons. 90% off and it even includes equipment rental. He wants me to come with him and he even offers to pay for my half. As incredible as that deal is I still make objections.

I don't know anything about scuba diving.
I don't have a wet suit.
I'm not sure it's safe. What if I can't breathe?

What if I panic?
and on and on.

Even if you're offering an incredible deal, you've got a well known brand like Groupon and you've built urgency into your offer, you're still going to have to deal with a certain amount of objections. There's no way around it.

But why go around? Why not go through each objection?

We have objections for every conversion or transaction. Every list we opt into, every product we plan to buy comes with at least a few objections. Instead of waiting for customers to spring them on us why not bring them up ourselves?

Because that would kill our chances of making a sale!

Or would it? When a customer has an objection what do they normally do? They keep it inside, they hide it. Sure they may mention a few but at a certain point, social pressure and insecurity kicks in, making it harder for your customer to spill the beans. They're likely to feel bad if they unload all of their objections on to you. So they hem and haw. They procrastinate and they put off making a decision.

But procrastination and decision making depend on urgency.

If they need your product now, if they're desperate, they'll call, email or text. They'll spill the beans and share their objections. This is good news. Their objections show you there are gaps in your marketing. There are unanswered questions, giving you an opportunity to fix the problem.

But instead of dealing with the objections we act like they don't exist.

Or we try to dodge objections when they appear, hoping if we ignore them customers will pull out their wallets and purses and just buy anyway. The irony is that hiding or deflecting the objection is actually what kills the sale.

So how do we defuse the objections and win the sale?

You start with a list. Take your time and list every possible objection a customer can make. Then list the answer to each of those specific objections with a detailed and logical response. When a customer mentions a new variation, add it to your list.

Do you really need a list of objections?

In a face to face meeting, a customer brings up the objections giving you an opportunity to defuse them right then and there. There's no chance of that happening online. Even worse, there's no way for you to know which objections will be brought up by each individual customer. Creating a list means you're prepared. You have a chance to tell the whole story, giving buyers the chance to find the objections that matter to them.

But the objections aren't just for the customer.

Every transaction has an influencer, a person your customer goes to for advice. Whenever we buy something we usually talk to someone we trust to get a second opinion. *"How does this look on me?"* Sometimes that influencer has nothing to say, other times they'll present your customer with objections they hadn't thought. *"It looks great on you but is it worth paying that much?"*

This kind of advice can give your customers cold feet.

But if you've prepared for and defused all of the main objections to your product or service, something beautiful happens.

If your customer has gone through your list they'll begin to counter and defuse each new objection that's mentioned. Your buyer begins to sell others on your product or service. Once they've taken this step they've publicly and psychologically committed themselves to buying.

And if they're not committed? What if they're non-buyers pretending to be interested?

This isn't so much of an objections issue as it is a target profile issue. If you've selected a target profile with the interest and willingness to buy what you're selling and you've identified real problems in your target profile interviews this should be rare.

If it's not and you're attracting a lot of these non-buyers it's an indication that **(a.)** you're using push marketing and **(b.)** you're targeting the wrong people. An endless stream of objections can be a clear cut sign that you're pushing something they don't want.

And how exactly are you supposed to find these objections?

The easiest way to find these objections is to ask. You can ask your customers and potential customers. You can ask your sales team. Talk with vendors and partners. The more you defuse, the less customers have to worry about and the more prepared they are to defuse influencer objections.

It's worth repeating that in most cases your customer is already interested in whatever it is you're offering. But they'll hesitate and that's normal. It's important for you to go through each of their objections in detail. And whatever you do, don't rush customers through their objections.

Because a rushed customer is a remorseful customer

It can be frustrating to work with slow buyers. But rushing them creates regret. Each buyer needs to sort through each of the objections and fears in their head. Doing this gives them a chance to resolve each one so they're fully convinced.

When they're rushed these objections aren't resolved. They're still in their head floating around. And it's these unresolved objections, these issues that drive customers to ask for their money back. And those that don't, remember. It's this memory that makes them hesitant to buy from you in the future.

And that hesitation, that reluctance, is not the future you want

When you lay out and defuse each objection, you give customers the comfort and freedom they need to continue the buying process. At this point, your customer is looking for more. There's no uncertainty as they move towards making a decision and there's no "I'm interested but..." This is assuming that what you're selling already exists.

Well, what if what you're offering doesn't exist?

Our ideas, products and services tend to be upgrades on what's already available. Smartphones improving on the cell phone. Bagless vacuums that don't lose suction replacing vacuums with bags. These are improvements on what we had before so our perceptions and past experiences are still the tools we'll rely on when it comes to objections.

If I launched my Aquatic Taekwondo class, your perception or past experience with traditional Taekwondo would inform your objections. You'd use what you know about traditional Taekwondo as a point of reference. Once that happens you get all of the past experience, perception and need to know a customer has in their head. If I wanted to invite you to join my class I'd have to use the traditional approach as a way to explain my new idea.

The problem comes when products and services are too far ahead of their time.

Which means that these products are probably going to fail. Let's look at an example.

QUBE.

QUBE was launched in 1977 as a cable platform. As a company QUBE was innovative, introducing new concepts like pay-per-view programs. When they started, their goal was simple.

"

"To create a faster method for groups to communicate and interact across distance."

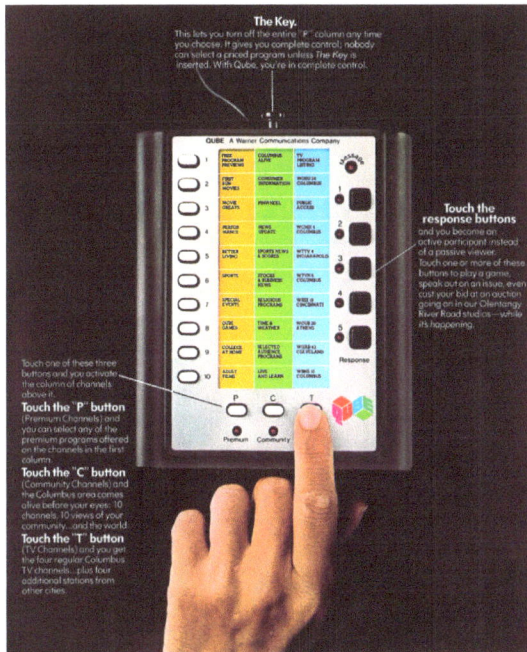

Consumers had a genuine need to know, but QUBE couldn't handle the objections

Source: http://www.gsbrown.org/compuserve/compuserve-on-qube-1981-07/

Their cable box allowed viewers to participate with others and share feedback while watching television, way back in the 70s. Wanted to share what you thought about the president's state of the union speech? QUBE made it possible. Looking for something to watch? QUBE pay-per-view made it easy.

But then there were objections.

Privacy concerns became a problem with consumers. They learned that their personal information, political views and even family interests could be stored in a database indefinitely. Then consumers discovered that the answers and information they shared could be traced back to them. Then there were concerns about hackers. The objections started to pile up and there simply wasn't enough information to counteract it. So customers stopped renewing, ultimately bringing QUBE to an end.[1]

QUBE shows us why your product needs to build on other products and services in the marketplace. When you building on the familiar, customers have something to connect with, to relate to. Once they relate to something familiar, their past experiences, perceptions and need to know follows.

Remember, objections are inevitable. When customers become interested, the objections are sure to follow. Defuse them ahead of time so customers can finish the buying process. Hide the objections and risk losing the sale.

Summary

Objections are inevitable

- Customers object to protect. They don't want to make a mistake so they create objections.

- Objections show a customer is interested. If they weren't interested they'd say no, nothing or leave. It shows they're aware of the risks involved.

- Objections come from three sources. Our past, our perceptions and our inexperience.

- Bring up and defuse each objection with a logical answer. Tell the whole story and explain things in detail.

- Ask for objections. Recruit customers, staff members and vendors to build your list. Defuse them one by one.

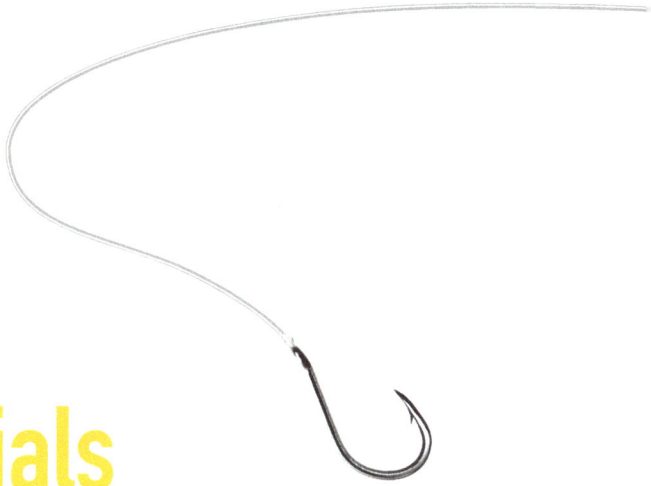

Testimonials

Why customers distrust them, how to make yours trustworthy

Alex and Paul were swamped with work.
New clients were streaming in and they simply couldn't keep up with demand. As a result their performance started to lag. Consequences of the problems they were having started to show.

They needed help. It was time to hire.

Alex posted their job openings and they watched as the resumes started to pour in. As they looked them over they noticed a trend.

They all talked a great game.

Each resume painted a rosy, one-sided picture of the applicant. Flawless work histories, extensive education, no negative reviews or failures and a love for every job and employer they ever had. Naturally, Alex and Paul were skeptical.

Paul was shocked. "You know, I'm pretty sure some of these people are stretching the truth. Some of these resumes are loaded with BS."

Alex chuckled. "Seems pretty standard to me."

So they did what smart businesses do. They started fact checking, calling old bosses and co-workers. They vetted and verified their applicants. There's two sides to every story and a resume only gives us one.

Resumes and testimonials have that in common as they're both one sided.

For the most part, testimonials are loaded with fluff and flattery. So we have trouble believing them. Take a look at the testimonials on LinkedIn. The majority of them are filled with flattery and praise but they lack substance. Every experience is ideal, every idea grand and every person's performance flawless. But that's not how it works in your head or in real life.

Read through too many testimonials like these and distrust starts to grow. These kind of testimonials aren't helpful.

And we all know why.

Everything is perfect, there's no problem, no doubt, no struggle. Naturally, most of us are skeptical after reading a bed of rosy testimonials. Something about all these rosy testimonials just doesn't sit well with us. We don't think they're believable and, after awhile, we start to gloss over them - or ignore them all together. Instead of getting you to buy, these testimonials have actually created resistance.

Rosy testimonials create resistance? How?

In the form of conscious or subconscious questions we ask ourselves, in the doubt they create. When we come across a collection of rosy testimonials we ask ourselves some questions.

- Is this testimonial authentic; is this person's experience real?
- Are these testimonials biased? Because they sound that way.
- This kind of success sounds crazy, can I expect the same results? Is that even possible?
- Did these things really happen?
- I read it but I still don't know what this testimonial is about. What are they selling again?

Testimonials are supposed to relieve our objections and calm our fears. And while the average testimonial helps somewhat, a large number of them don't. Because the testimonials that start, continue, and end with praise tend to produce the opposite of what they were meant to do. Which makes it hard to establish credibility.

Then what makes a testimonial believable or credible?

Testimonials that show both sides to the story. When we're thinking about buying something we need reassurance. And it's a big step because we're choosing where we'll invest our trust. So we look for social proof in the form of testimonials. And while the average testimonial reassures us a bit, they don't relieve the fear and doubt in our minds.

When they're believable, testimonials lead with fear, doubt or resistance. They describe the fears and doubts your customers are already thinking about. Which is what we do when we recommend a product or service. Take these real testimonials for example.

Testimonial #1

"I've worked with countless web hosts over the years, knowing that each time I migrate from one provider to another, it's going to be painful. With Synthesis, that migration pain never came — leaving me with time to focus on what I do best: run my business, not rule the infrastructure that enables me to run my business. I wish they were around in 1996 when I started. Could've saved me a lot of resources!" [1]

Testimonial #2

"Even with numerous friends that swear by their Roomba, I was still skeptical. How could this little machine really clean enough to impress me?

...My final opinion on the Roomba is that it definitely exceeded my expectations on its cleaning ability. It's intuitiveness, style and ease of use also impressed me and the four stars that I've giving it are well earned!" [2]

Testimonial #3

"

"We had been in quest of a designer for several months, but the few ones I got in touch with never seemed able to meet our taste. Finally, when I discovered David through a Google search, it appeared likely that such a passionate designer would be the partner we had been looking for — which became obvious as soon as we started working together.

After reviewing our requirements, David sent us a few proposals and, taking great care, created numerous modifications. We were plainly satisfied. Most importantly, each modification introduced that special detail that makes all the difference. Needless to say we are extremely satisfied with the results." [3]

See the doubt and skepticism in the beginning of each of those?

When you lead with customer doubts and fears your testimonials become believable, something others can relate to. So if your testimonial were a candy bar, fear and doubt would be the milk chocolate covering on the outside, the nuts would be the answer to the objection and praise would be the creamy nougat in the middle.

The praise in your testimonials needs a light coating of fear and doubt.

As we've seen, we're drawn to problems. We hunt for them and obsessively seek them out. So the doubts, the problems - they come first. When they do, they give your testimonials credibility. They're more believable, it's not just flattery and fluff. It's a story, about the fears and doubts your customer had and how you relieved them.

But stories, like candy bars, need to be crafted.

Baked doesn't mean that you're going to create an imaginary story. It also doesn't mean that you're going to stretch the truth or lie.

If you're a confectioner, you need to follow a formulaic process if you want your candy to feel and taste the same each time. Mix your ingredients in the wrong order, over cook your caramel and suddenly things don't taste right. It's the same with testimonials. When you use the right formula, your testimonials become specific. Follow the recipe and you'll get specific, consistent and repeatable results.

Getting specific or consistent feedback from customers is tough though isn't it?

Customers are often too busy to give a testimonial. And when you find someone that's willing to share, they can't seem to figure out what to say. The ones that get around to writing seem to write something that's boring or loaded with flattery. A good testimonial can be hit or miss.

Waiting makes it harder too. The longer you wait to ask for a testimonial the harder it will be for customers to remember anything. They're more likely to forget the fears, doubts, facts, and results that make great testimonials so powerful.

How's a recipe supposed to help you create testimonials with problems like those?

It's simple. You ask for them when the experience is still fresh and you use the recipe. The recipe is simply a list of questions that keep your customers mind on the right track. Ask the right questions and your testimonials have all the fear, doubt, praise and story elements baked in.

Questions you should ask[4]

1. What obstacle would have prevented you from buying?

Customers always have an obstacle or perception. It could be an issue with the terms, delivery, money or something else. As we've learned, objections are a normal part of the process. Asking this question shines a light on the issue which is great for two reasons. First, they'll tell you about the biggest obstacle in the way. And second, they'll share perspectives on the issues and obstacles in a way you may not have thought of.

This is even more important when other customers are dealing with the same obstacle.

2. What did you find as a result of buying this?

This question defuses the objection in question 1 using the customer's own words. There's no doubt in their mind that their purchase was worth it, even with the obstacles. Question 1 exposes the problem, question 2 provides an answer.

3. Which feature did you like most about our product or service?

Getting customers to focus on a single feature is important. It keeps them on track and prevents confusion, enabling you to get a whole lot of detail and context on what that single feature has done for them.

4. What would be three other benefits to this product or service?

Once you've drilled deep with that single feature, you can go wide by asking about three additional benefits they've experienced by using your product or service.

5. Would you recommend this to someone else? If so, why?

With this question, customers put their credibility on the line. When they recommend you to someone else they're stating they trust and believe in you. When they share the reasons for their belief they make a psychological commitment.

6. Anything else you'd like to share?

It's easier to share and go in-depth during an in-person or phone conversation. There's a certain flow, a back-and-forth exchange, that makes sharing very natural. Sometimes customers have something important they're waiting to share with you. They tend to be polite so this question gives them the permission they need to open up a bit. This question is not as effective when customers are writing in.

This recipe, the structure we use to craft our testimonials actually works to defuse objections. The obstacles customers mention in question one is actually the objection.

So our testimonials are meant to answer and defuse objections. [5]

Let's use one of the testimonials we looked at earlier. First, the fear and doubt we ask about in question one:

> *"I've worked with countless web hosts over the years, knowing that each time I migrate from one provider to another, it's going to be painful..."*

Next we see how fear and doubt, the objection, is defused as the customer shares their experience. Notice how they talk about the best feature of a server migration - more time to focus on their business, and not the tools they use to run their business.

> *"...With Synthesis, that migration pain never came — leaving me with time to focus on what I do best: run my business, not rule the infrastructure that enables me to run my business..."*

While an explicit recommendation would've made this testimonial rock solid, they've done a great job finding and defusing the objection. They go on to discuss some additional benefits and they talk a little more about the kind of experience they've had since they started.

> *"I wish they were around in 1996 when I started. Could've saved me a lot of resources!"*

Great testimonials as we've seen are crafted. When they follow a specific recipe, the results are consistently great.[6] When customers defuse their own objections, they relieve the same fears and doubts in others. But what happens when customers don't have the same objections you're looking to answer? Is there a way to control the topic?

How to control the topic of your testimonial.

You don't control the topic, you guide it. That sounds like bad news doesn't it? How are your testimonials supposed to defuse customer objections if you can't even control the objection they bring up?

What you can do is give them a structure to follow. So let's say your top three objections are price, delivery, and warranty. Offer those three topics as bait. If these topics are a problem for them they'll bite. You can go from there, asking the appropriate questions.

And if they have a different objection? Roll with it. If you present the topics you thought were the big objections and they bring up something else, follow their train of thought. Why you ask?

Because that train of thought is taking you to a new objection. One you either haven't thought of or one you felt wasn't as much of a concern. Worst case scenario it's an obscure objection you decide not to use. If that happens you can always talk with clients about the big topics.

Sure, you could come up with a story yourself but customers would see right through it. When customers share their story, they share all of the gory details, emotions, awkwardness and nuances they remember. The more recent the experience the more detailed and emotional the response. This makes their story believable and real, something we're all able to recognize and identify with.

Testimonials as we've seen, have a clear and distinct purpose; to defuse objections and build trust. And that's important because it enables customers to continue with their decision making process. Once this happens the perceived risk in a customer's mind is reduced but not eliminated. To remove risk you need Risk Reversals.

Summary

Why you need Testimonials

- People view testimonials with skepticism. Most testimonials are one-sided, painting a rosy, unrealistic picture of what it's like to be a customer. We tend to disbelieve them.

- When people share testimonials, they lead with the negatives. Statements like: *"Remember that shady looking strip mall on the smelly side of town?"* are used to draw attention to the problem.

- Customers defuse the objections by sharing an experience that counteracts or contradicts the objection. *"When I went inside was pretty shocked. That strip mall didn't look anything like the outside. Everything was bright, colorful and it smelled great. I even got name brand items at 90% off in their outlet mall."*

- You "craft" great testimonials by following the recipe. The recipe consists of six specific questions that you use to guide customers, keeping their train of thought focused. This makes it easy for them to answer your questions when you.

- While you can't control the topic of their testimonial, you can present options to your customer as bait. If these topics are a problem they'll bite. If they don't, just roll with it.

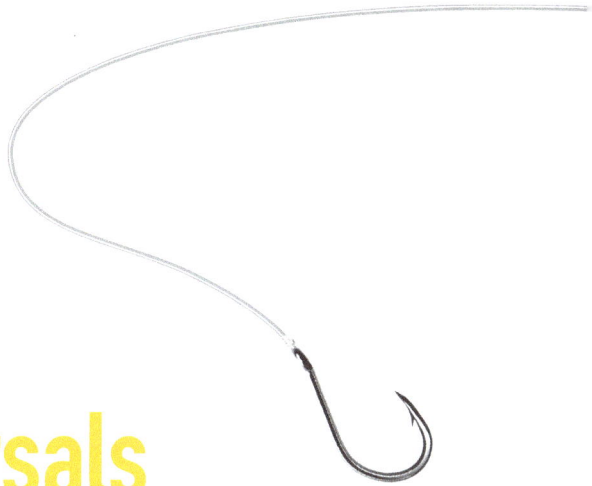

Risk Reversals

Why we struggle to seal the deal

"I'm sorry, but that's too much of a risk for us to take. We're gonna have to pass."

Alex was crushed.

He'd spent the last four weeks negotiating with Nathan. He asked questions and pointed out problems, sharing his ideas on how Nathan could fix several bottlenecks in his business. Nathan was pumped.

But there was a problem.

"I'm really concerned about delivery. Will you guys be able to deliver what I need on time?" Nathan stared as he waited for an answer.

Alex swallowed hard. "Of course! We're just as interested in finishing on time as you are."

But he could see that Nathan wasn't convinced. He knew it was important, but he didn't think it was a deal breaker. Even though he couldn't see them, the signs were there, staring Alex in the face. What he needed was an answer. He needed a way to reduce the risk customers felt. He needed a risk reversal.

A risk reversal, what's that?

Josh Kaufman, in his book The Personal MBA, defines it best:

> *"Risk Reversal is a strategy that transfers some (or all) of the risk of a transaction from the buyer to the seller. The seller agrees to make things right in advance if the purchaser doesn't end up satisfied."* [1]

It's a way for you the seller to eliminate the barriers and deal breakers that keep a customer from buying. And when it comes to buying, we're all worried about risk.

What are we so worried about though?

At its core, risk is about fear. Customers are afraid of looking stupid, making a mistake, losing money and a whole lot of other things. When they meet you for the first time they're skeptical. *"I don't know you, I don't trust you, why should I work with you?"* And while we know you're a good person who'd never intentionally set out to harm your customer, they don't know that.

Yet this fear is part of our decision-making process. It's our brain's way of protecting us. And this fear, while helpful, creates a huge amount of pressure. Pressure that has to be released before a customer feels comfortable enough to buy from you. Well, where do these fears come from then?

From the same place we get our objections.

They come from our past experiences, perceptions and inexperience. These three areas shape and inform our fears. We all hate painful experiences. They're not enjoyable so being the reasonable people we are, we look for ways to minimize and avoid them.

But the problem with most transactions is that both buyer and seller bring these fears to the table with them. Sellers spend their time focusing on closing the deal and/or avoiding pain. This creates a problem. If the seller's focused on their issues, who's focused on relieving the buyer's fears?

The buyer.

And how do they respond in that scenario? They keep a tight grip on their wallets.

They push for all kinds of concessions in an effort to reduce the fear they feel. They haggle and they fuss about price.

Many of them aren't even consciously aware of why they're afraid.

And most businesses stumble because they expect their customers to shoulder all of the risk. Yet when the roles are reversed things are different. They suddenly want everything they've paid for.

Which is where risk reversal comes in.

There are two components to a risk reversal. Sean D'Souza calls them the obvious risk and the hidden risk.[2]

Obvious Risk:
The Marcinko family purchased a brand-new Chevy Equinox. Almost immediately, their vehicle began to stall at the most random times and places. It stalled in the middle of the intersection and on the highway, turning their car into a safety hazard. The Marcinkos said they tried to get it repaired at the dealer where they bought it but after four attempts, it was still an issue. So GM offered to buy back the car.[3]

This is an example of the obvious risk. You buy a product or service and there's a chance that it won't work, that it'll break, that something will go wrong.

Hidden:
Then there's GM's company, OnStar. OnStar does a lot. "Subscription based communications, in-vehicle security, hands free calling, turn-by-turn navigation, and remote diagnostics systems available throughout the United States, Canada and China".

Whew.

If you're familiar with OnStar, the hidden risk has probably crossed your mind. *What if they're spying on me? What if they're recording everything I do and everywhere I go?* It's the fear that if you buy a car equipped with OnStar, your privacy is gone. It's something that crops up whenever a new customer is asked to buy.

And this isn't the only hidden risk GM faces.

Yet, when these trust issues crop up GM faces them openly.

Privacy is a sticky issue, but GM does their best to reverse customer risk. They state (in detail) how OnStar works, the information they collect and what they do with it. They tell you about your rights, how to know when OnStar connects with your car and that OnStar Advisors are also required to "announce their presence immediately once they have established voice communication into a vehicle".[4]

They offer a 60 day "love it or return it" money back guarantee on all 2012 and 2013 Chevrolet models.[5] Don't like Chevy or OnStar? Simply return the car for a full refund. What if you purchased a used car? GM offers a three day 150 mile satisfaction guarantee on any certified pre-owned Chevy, Buick or GMC.[6]

Their no-haggle sales price, called Total Confidence Pricing, means customers get a fixed, non-negotiable price that's lower than retail.

But GM tends to spark political debate

So let's suspend politics for a bit here and think like a new customer. Imagine you're in the market for a new car. Let's say you're in a foreign country and you need a vehicle. You've looked around for a while but you've decided on a Diahatsu Charade or a TATA Indica.

Source: http://motoburg.com

Source: http://carsfolia.com

The risks are there regardless of who sells it

Let's also pretend these vehicles have the same features and the same potential risks. Which do you prefer? The one that removes all of the risk to you the customer, or the one that makes the usual offer?

The answer is obvious.

Most of us would be willing to pay a premium for the right risk reversals, if they reduced our risk. Yet most businesses avoid them. Why?

Because all of your customers will ask for their money back.

And if your product or service has major problems they should. When IKEA discovered their almond cakes might contain poo, they were forced to recall thousands of cakes in 23 countries.[7] That seems like the obvious choice to make, right?

Most of us don't want to eat poo. And most of us have seen product recalls before. Virtually all of us have requested refunds on purchases we've made. And while we've chosen a dramatic example to make a point, the reality is really quite different.

Customers asking for a refund is really quite rare. It's hard for most people to do because that's admitting they've made a mistake. Most people prefer to simply stop doing business with you and disappear quietly, never to be seen again. The reason? We don't want to look stupid and we're socially conditioned to be passive, to be nice.[8]

Which is why risk reversals are the canaries in the coal mine.

If customers request refunds en masse, you need to fix something. If you notice an increase in complaints or refund requests, something is wrong. Because most of the time, customers prefer not to say anything.

So while it's unpleasant when customers complain, it's actually a good thing. They want you to fix the problem. They want you to make it right. Knowing what the problem is, that they want a refund, gives you a chance to fix it; so even if it's bad news, it's good news to know.

When you have risk reversals, recalls and refunds should be the exception, not the rule.

But when it comes to profits, the opposite is true. When you transfer the risk from buyers to yourself, profits go up. Your business begins to achieve lofty goals. Customers begin to take action once the risk to them is gone. Suddenly they're willing to pay a premium for your product or service. They're willing to compete for your attention.

Won't risk reversals make you look desperate?

Doesn't it cheapen your product, service or brand? It's a legitimate question. So let's take a look at Zappos for the answer.

Zappos.com sells shoes online. Lots and lots of shoes. If you've purchased shoes online before, you know it's a risky ordeal. What if I'm unhappy with my shoes? Can I return them? Shipping makes this more expensive, I'll just buy it from my local store. Can I return these shoes after 30 days?

Zappos builds their risk reversal around these core fears.

FREE Shipping:

Zappos.com offers free shipping on all domestic orders placed on our website, with no minimum order sizes or special exceptions.

Just because shipping is free doesn't mean it should take a long time. Zappos.com understands that getting your items quickly is important to you, so we make every effort to process your order quickly. When you order from our website, you can expect to receive your order within 4-5 business days.

FREE Returns:

If you are not 100% satisfied with your purchase, you can return your order to the warehouse for a full refund (Returns must be unworn, in the state you received them, and in the original packaging). We believe that in order to have the best possible online shopping experience, our customers should not have to pay for domestic return shipping. So if for whatever reason you're not happy with your purchase, just go through our easy self-service return process (via My Account) to print out a free return label - your domestic shipping costs are prepaid.

With Zappos Retail, Inc.'s 365 day return policy, there are no special catches or exceptions. All we ask is that you send the items back to us in the original packaging, and make sure that the merchandise is in the same condition. [9]

And how do customers feel about the Zappos Free Return Policy? Do they think it's desperate or pathetic? Let's take a look at some shopper comments: [10]

❝

"Zappos actually has a 365 day return policy. You can send back shoes within a year of buying them as long as they are like new. I have used them for several pairs of shoes and will continue to. They even let you know when they receive the return. Their customer service is outstanding! I can't compliment them enough."

❝

"Shipping and return costs are ultimately what drives my selection between online retailers. I use BN.com over Amazon in ordering books because BN is "fast and free shipping" policy where I receive my items in 2-3 days versus 2-3 weeks with Amazon's shipping option. Zappos wins out b/c it does not cost me anything to return the items and initial shipping is super fast.

Customer service does ultimately win out over price when it comes to my online shopping."

❝

"Zappos gets a lot of my business, precisely because of its policies (okay, the shoes are sexy, well-made and comfortable too). Zappos is second only to a Nordstrom's clearance sale."

and finally...

❝

"Zappos is undoubtedly doing great business. Not only will your shoe shoppers delight with their buys but will also have a shipping-worry-free shopping as well. And if there's something wrong with their purchase, they have all year to return it. Just amazing."

So not only does Zappos attract more customers with their policies, but the word desperate doesn't even come into play. One customer mentions that competitors have even started *copying* Zappos' return policies. I think that's good evidence that risk reversals are neither cheap nor desperate.

But those are products. Can risk reversals work with services?

It's painful to replace a product. You may not be able to sell returned items at full price but if it's in good condition you can make some money on it. No such luck if you're selling a service. If you offer a service, you're selling your time. Once that's gone, it's gone. So how are risk reversals supposed to work if you offer services?

You compartmentalize.

Separate each piece of the project or service and reverse the risk. Let's say you're a writer. Customers may want certain results from your writing. They want excellent grammar. A certain amount of words. A certain level of quality. But that would be a lot to wrap up in one risk reversal.

So you focus on them separately.

Are customers afraid your work will be filled with poor grammar? Guarantee grammar to reverse the risk. Do customers have specific quality expectations? Show them how you'll take on any risks to meet their expectations. When you break things up into smaller pieces you minimize your risk, making it easier for customers to respond. Take proactive steps to fix the problem on your dime. What if you do all of that and they're still afraid to move forward?

That means there's still risk involved.

You'll need to dig deeper and find the real reason for their fear. It could be something you've missed, a fear they're afraid or embarrassed to share or simply that they distrust your risk reversal. Which is a problem that tends to crop up when someone they trust (you, a competitor or someone before you) failed to deliver on a promise made in the past.

That's a problem because risk reversals need to show that you're proactive.

And that you're willing to put your money where your mouth is and stand behind your product or service. Risk reversals make *"that's too much of a risk to take"* a thing of the past. Customers know there's nothing to fear because you're willing to take the hit to keep them safe. And that makes you trustworthy.

It doesn't however make you unique, which is important if we want customers to actually complete the order process. Neglect that and customers will continue to leave you for someone else.

Summary
We need Risk Reversals to seal the deal

- Customers are afraid. Sometimes they know why, other times they don't.

- Doing business is risky. Most of the time customers are expected to take on all of the risk. This makes their fear worse.

- There are two kinds of risks. The obvious risk and the hidden risk. Both need to be addressed if a customer's fears will be relieved.

- Risk Reversals transfer the risks from the buyer to the seller.

- Risk Reversals are the canaries in the coal mine. Asking for a refund is just as uncomfortable for customers as it is for you. If refunds become the norm something is very wrong.

- Customers don't see Risk Reversals as desperate. It's actually the opposite, they're amazed and excited by those that offer them.

- Risk reversals should show that you're proactive. Show customers that you're willing to stand behind your product or service.

Uniqueness

Convincing customers you're the only one for them

"You guys are all the same."

Alex squirmed in his seat.

"Everyone in your industry is basically offering the same thing. You sell the same stuff and you're offering the same terms, give or take a few paragraphs."

Alex thought about Jess and her warning, a few weeks earlier.

If you do everything I've told you but ignore what makes you unique, customers will leave. They'll demand the same things you're offering from someone else and they'll get it. Why would they need you if they can get what you're offering from someone else?

Jim came to Alex three weeks ago. Almost immediately, he was interested in what Alex had to say. Alex felt he'd learned from his mistakes with Nathan. Things were going well. *This deal's in the bag*, he had told himself.

Jim pumped him for information and now he seemed ready to dump him. Jim's voice snapped Alex back to the present.

"So I'm not sure why I should pay you 15% more when I can get it from Graham or my guy for less."

Alex choked as he started to answer. He cleared his throat as he stalled for time.

"Well Jim, we really care about your business. We focus on each client and we won't treat you like a number."

Jim chuckled.

"That's funny because Ivy over at Paragon made me the same promise last week. Look, I hate to cut things short but I've got another meeting. Lemme get back to you next week, alright?"

"Sure, I'll call Susan to set something up". But Alex knew better. He'd never hear from Jim again.

We're all like Jim in a way. We all have these perceptions.

It's the stigma, *when you've seen one you've seen em' all*. It's a common assumption, but this perception creates a catch 22 since customers expect uniqueness. Some of them ask about your uniqueness outright. Which is a smart move, because most of time, they can't tell the difference between you or your competitors.

Most businesses can't tell the difference either.

When you've seen one, you've seen em' all is a stigma that businesses subconsciously accept. Most of us don't have a clue about what makes us unique. So we accept this perception that we're not unique, not special. And that hurts. Sure we try to think of something. But what comes out looks generic. We can't all have the widest selection or lowest prices. How many businesses make bland statements like "we guarantee your satisfaction" or "we care about our customers"? So we're left with meaningless labels that are neither special nor unique.

Because we followed bad advice.

Experts told you how important it was to be unique. "Find your USP!"[1] they hollered. And when you asked about how to find it they confused you even more. Ask your customers, the same ones that have a hard time telling you and your competitors apart. Ask your vendors. Ask your employees.

And as you ask, you feel yourself going from I dunno to I'm confused.

Some give you generic answers filled with words like "satisfaction", "service" or "selection". Which seems helpful at first until you realize that your competitors can (and do) say the same exact things. Others struggle to give you any answer at all. They sputter and stumble as they try to think of something. Then there's the list givers. They give you a list of things that make you unique, confusing you even more. Which one do you pick?

At this point we do what most businesses do.

We pick one and try to make it work. We choose something safe, something nice that won't offend anyone. Or we accept the stigma, believe the lie and simply move on. After all, *when you've seen one you've seen em' all.*

But you know better.

It doesn't matter if you're a plumber, realtor or personal trainer. At some level you know that you're different. You use different methods from your competitors, your focus is different, your approach is different, your process is different. You can't help but be unique.

So why is it so hard to find what makes you unique?

Because we're trying to find it. It's the process, the technique that we use to find our uniqueness that makes things difficult. Because we're digging through our past to find some incredible thing that makes us unique. And as we dig through our past we fear that we'll never find the one thing that makes us unique.

And we're right, because uniqueness doesn't come from our past, it comes from our future.

In 1962, Frederick W. Smith wrote a paper for an economics class, laying out his plan for an overnight delivery service (the first of its kind) in the information age. Folklore has it he got a C for his paper because his professor thought his idea was unfeasible.

Frederick continued to develop his idea, and his company, Federal Express, became known for the slogan "FedEx: When your package absolutely, positively has to get there overnight." [2] But here's the interesting part.

Frederick Smith pulled his uniqueness out of thin air.

When he created the idea, he had no company, no business and no support. He had no past history to refer to, no success stories he could use. He hadn't made a single sale at that point but his uniqueness was ready.

When we create uniqueness we usually ask, what's special or unique about my business? But to create uniqueness we need to look to the future. We need to ask ourselves the question: "What do I want to be known for? What do I want to do in my business that no one else does?" Because uniqueness comes from looking to the future and making a stand.

So you'll have to invent your uniqueness, just like Frederick did with FedEx.

Picture your business in the future. Paint a rosy picture in your head of what your successful business looks like. What's the one thing your business is known for?

Is it the fastest? The most accurate? Is it the most profitable? Choose the one thing you'd like your business to be known for. But whatever you stand for, be sure it's just one thing and not two or three.

Because you can't stand for more than one thing and still be unique.

Google offers more than 120 products but they're known for just one thing. Search. They state their uniqueness clearly on their about page.

"

"We do search. With one of the world's largest research groups focused exclusively on solving search problems, we know what we do well, and how we could do it better. Through continued iteration on difficult problems, we've been able to solve complex issues and provide continuous improvements to a service that already makes finding information a fast and seamless experience for millions of people. Our dedication to improving search helps us apply what we've learned to new products, like Gmail and Google Maps. Our hope is to bring the power of search to previously unexplored areas, and to help people access and use even more of the ever-expanding information in their lives." [3]

They've taken a stand and staked their entire business on their uniqueness so much, the phrase "Google it" has become a verb, making the brand name "Google" ubiquitous with search. Most of us understand that "Google it" means to look something up on the Internet (regardless of the search engine you actually use).

Google's uniqueness tells us two things about uniqueness in general.

First, it makes your offering simple and easy for people to understand.

How do we know people understand Google's uniqueness? By the widespread use of the phrase "Google it". In fact, *"Google it"* and it's variants, *Let me Google that for you*, *LMGTFY* and *just Google it yourself* have become cultural shorthand. When we tell someone to Google it, they know exactly what we mean. We understand Google's uniqueness, which means we're able to share it. Persuasion is a byproduct of clarity. Uniqueness creates that clarity.

Second, your uniqueness becomes the blueprint for your business.

It narrows your focus, giving you a clear path to pursue. Google's 120 products? All a result of their uniqueness, their focus on search.[4]

> *"Our dedication to improving search helps us apply what we've learned to new products, like Gmail and Google Maps. Our hope is to bring the power of search to previously unexplored areas, and to help people access and use even more of the ever-expanding information in their lives."*

The vast majority of the 120+ products Google releases depends on search directly or indirectly. More than half of them use search prominently.

Third, your customers, competitors and the media begin to see you as different.

Early search engines were problematic; the results they returned were hit or miss. The results just weren't relevant enough. Alta Vista, one of the more popular search engines at the time, struggled to answer plain English queries like "Where can I find a map of Ethiopia?" So they tried to put a Band-Aid on the problem while they figured things out. They offered a "freshness guarantee", stating that their index was refreshed every 28 days.[5]

Then along came Google.

From the beginning Larry Page and Sergey Brin tackled a big problem. The information search engines provided wasn't relevant. This made searching difficult. Google was their answer to the relevance problem.

It didn't take long before customers and media outlets began taking notice. PC mag reported that Google *"has an uncanny knack for returning extremely relevant results. There's much more to come at Google, but even in its prototype form it's a great search engine."* [6]

Fast forward to today and Google's rosy picture has come true. All of us understand Google's uniqueness. Want accurate and relevant search results? Google it. It's become a verb we share, that we use to provide instructions to those too lazy to Google it themselves.

Yet uniqueness, by itself, is not enough.

Because we have to be told about uniqueness. We'd never know that Google returned ultra relevant results or that FedEx guaranteed overnight delivery until we were told (by someone or through experience). Your uniqueness is no different, if you want the benefits that come with being unique, people need to know about it first. Share it with customers, on your website, via social media, in your presentations and in your downloads. Share your uniqueness wherever you speak with customers.

But you need to be sure that customers are getting the right message.

Are you really unique? Do customers know what makes you unique? How can you tell? By asking of course. Ask a customer about what makes you unique. If they can't tell you what it is immediately, it means you don't have your uniqueness in place, or you haven't made it well known. In either case, there's work to be done.

If your uniqueness can be applied to any other business, and there's no confusion, it's not unique.

Generic statements you can apply to any business:

- We have 15 years of experience

- We guarantee your satisfaction

- We have the _____ selection of _____

- We put our customers first

When you're truly unique, that uniqueness applies to you and only you. What comes to mind when you read the uniqueness below?

1. Melts in your mouth, not in your hand

2. You get a fresh, hot pizza delivered to your door in 30 min or it's free

3. When your package, absolutely, positively has to get there overnight

4. Drive safely[7]

See the difference? Generic statements at the top are just that, generic. Anyone can say them and there's nothing you can do to stop that.

True uniqueness on the other hand, is designed around a specific business, making a specific stand. Because of that it can be protected. Once you've done the work and you've created true uniqueness you protect it.

But let's be honest here. Who wants to do all of that work?

It's a scary thing to put yourself out there, to look to your future and make a stand for something. Your uniqueness could force you to make a promise, to create expectations. What if you fail? Wouldn't it be easier to just continue as is? Maybe we could put the other elements into place first and then deal with uniqueness later?

Just one problem.

You could take everything we've talked about so far and put them into place one by one. If you've combined all the elements we've talked about but you ignore uniqueness, all you've really done is prepared the customer to go to your competitors.

Because now, thanks to you, they're an educated customer. They know what they need. But without your uniqueness, you and your competitors are all the same to them. *Because when you've seen one, you've seen em' all.*

You know that's not true, but they don't. They don't know enough about you. Which is where uniqueness comes in.

So how do you create uniqueness?

In three simple steps.

1. Create a list of the things that make your business unique.

Brainstorm with your team. Talk it over with those you trust. It's a brainstorming session so it's important that you write down all of the ideas that are presented no matter how crazy or ridiculous they sound.

While it's not always the case, some of the ideas that sound ridiculous now can be viable later. Ability, circumstance, perceptions and resources can change.

2. Use a weighted ranking system to determine which one is most important

A weighted ranking system is best because it shows preference. This and not that. This is crucial because over time it becomes quite clear where our preferences lie.

3. Clarify, sharpen and simplify the winner.

Once you've identified what makes you unique, you'll need to provide more detail and drama. When Fred Smith created FedEx, he had his uniqueness in place. But FedEx didn't stop there. They went into great detail. They told us about how overnight delivery works, their delivery areas, service days, weight limitations and more. You'll need to provide the ins and outs of your uniqueness as well so it's crystal clear to customers.

Making things crystal clear requires specificity.

It's easy to put the work in and end up with something vague or generic. Imagine you'd like to buy a new home. A friend of yours introduces you to Shari, your new Realtor. You meet her for the first time and as she shakes your hand she tells you:

"I'm the best".

Almost immediately you start wonder.

The best at what?

Finding homes?
Negotiating price?
Selling homes?

The whole Realtor thing?
What does she mean by best?
How does she define best?

Because customers are looking for specifics, they want details.

Which is where most businesses stumble.

And Shari is no different here. She sticks with simply being "the best". Which is useless because it lacks specificity and context. So instead of being seen for the amazing professional she is, she's viewed with skepticism and forced to continue to haggle for her commissions.

Let's see how our three step process could have made things different for Shari.

What makes Shari, our Realtor unique?

1. Knows how to sell homes fast.

2. Knows how to attract buyers with money.

3. Great client rapport.

4. Connections in place to keep deals on track.

Weighted ranking system might have looked like this:

Knows how to sell homes fast. **(5 votes)**
Knows how to attract buyers with money. **(10 votes)**
Great client report. **(2 votes)**
Connections to make deals happen. **(3 votes)**

Clarify, sharpen and simplify the winner.

Shari's team decides to concentrate on "knows how to attract buyers with money". So she goes into considerable detail. She talks about how lots of people that typically come to Realtor open houses are tire kickers, either they're not interested in buying a home or they can't afford one.

She talks about how her open houses are always full, how 96% of the people at her open houses are buyers who are pre-approved for a loan. She tells you about her proprietary database of buyers and how she helps them qualify for a home loan. She talks about how she takes care of them before, during and after the sale. She shares their stories and talks about how loyal they are. And as she irons out the details, her uniqueness takes shape.

"129 buyers: ready to buy, before you're ready to sell."

With her uniqueness qualified, she's ready to tell customers about what makes her special. She knows where her focus needs to be and what drives her business. Thanks to specificity, she's able to avoid the "You're all the same" mentality completely. She has something customers can't get anywhere else.

Weighted Ranking, What's that?

When we need to make a decision on a list of items, we're often asked to choose or rank the items. The intent is usually to determine preference or desire so we're told to list them in the order of importance (e.g. 1 = most important, 3 = least important).

So what if I were give a choice between Ford, Toyota or Volkswagen?

1. Toyota

2. Volkswagen

3. Ford

A ranking system is a bad idea if we're trying to determine perference. What if my family had both a Toyota and a Volkswagen? It's quite possible I love both my imports equally. Ranking in order of importance means my preference creates a problem and I'm forced to choose (even though I don't want to).

Let's say we use a weighted ranking system. You give me 20 votes I can divvy up as I please. If I did that then I could tell you more about my preferences, like this:

Toyota **(9 votes)**
Volkswagen **(9 votes)**
Ford **(2 votes)**

My preference is suddenly more clear isn't it? It tells you that I love both my imports, while my interest in Ford is a distant second.

Summary
Why you need to be unique

- Uniqueness is a catch 22. Most customers have the perception that businesses are all the same, a photographer is a photographer. Yet customers look for and expect uniqueness.

- Finding uniqueness is hard because we try to find uniqueness. Asking customers and vendors isn't helpful because they try to "find it" as well.

- Creating uniqueness is easier than finding it. Look to your future and make a stand. What's the one thing you'd want to improve for your customers? The one thing you'd like to be known for?

- Uniqueness, by definition, points to a single, solitary example. Choose one thing and make that your focus. Own that one place in your customer's mind.

- Why you need uniqueness: It makes your offering simple and easy for people to understand. Your uniqueness becomes the blueprint for your business. Customers, competitors and the media begin to see you as different.

- Uniqueness needs to be shared. We need to be told about uniqueness. We'd never know about FedEx overnight shipping if we weren't told. It's the same for each of us. Share your uniqueness wherever you can.

- Ignoring uniqueness sets your customers up to leave. Creating uniqueness attracts customers to you.

- Creating uniqueness is a step-by-step ordeal. **1.** Make a big list of the things that make your business unique. **2.** Use a weighted ranking system to determine what's most important. **3.** Clarify, sharpen and simplify the winner.

Presentation

How ignoring it creates confusion, keeps customers from buying

Jess had just finished her assessment of the business. While Alex and Paul were overwhelmed, everything was suddenly clear: customers weren't buying because they weren't getting what they needed. They knew they needed to make some immediate changes.

Jess was way ahead of them. She arranged a meeting with Nick, her boyfriend and their new designer.

"I need you guys to talk with Nick. He'll take you through the things we've talked about."

Jess arranged for them to meet at Starbucks. When Alex arrived he realized that he'd never met Nick.

Great, just great. I forgot to ask Jess what he looks like. Now I have no idea who I'm meeting.

As he scanned the coffeehouse, he tried to identify those most likely to be Nick.

"Nick?"
"Huh? No sorry."

As he went from person to person, his embarrassment grew.

A voice behind him caught his ear.

"Alex ?"

He whirled around to see a long haired man wearing faded jeans and a black t-shirt, his arms and neck covered with tattoos. He pointed and asked, "Nick?"

"Not what you were expecting right?"

Alex tried to hold in his embarrassment but he felt his face flush. "I'm sorry, it's just tha-"

Nick cut him off with a laugh, "S'okay, I get that sometimes, no worries. Take a seat and let's get started."

Alex felt uncomfortable and embarrassed but he soon got over it and was able to work with Nick to come up with a plan. He vowed that this situation would never happen again. Alex had walked past Nick several times but never stopped to ask for his name.

Because his judgment was based on appearance.

And as we all know, looks and appearance matter a whole lot.[1] Like it or not, when we look at people, we make a number of instant assumptions and snap decisions. What they're like, their character and their trustworthiness. Whether we'll help, support or follow them.

We judge potential mates on their appearance. Politicians that are clean cut and put together are viewed as more competent and capable.[2] Job applicants that look the part tend to do well in interviews. People that drive fancy cars or wear name brand threads are viewed as rich or successful.

And to a certain extent we're usually right.

A 2009 study found that observers were able to accurately judge some aspects of a stranger's personality by simply looking at a photo of them. They then compared those judgments with those that knew the person in each photo and found their assessments were (in some areas) spot on.

Laura P. Naumann of the University of California, Berkeley wrote: "As we predicted, physical appearance serves as a channel through which personality is manifested." [3]

Our appearance is basically a canvas we paint our personality, values, tastes and temperament on.

Does the same thing apply to our digital appearance?

The answer is yes. We tend to put things in our websites and marketing that matter to us. We choose certain words and visuals because we want to be viewed a certain way. Some of us choose to share religious motivations for being in business, while for others it's deeply personal. Each of our sites show a personality blended with our presentation - regardless of whether we like that personality or not.

That's a lot of power and it's dangerous in the wrong hands.

Customers use presentation as an assessment tool. When customers visit your site for the first time, they go through a mental checklist as they rate your business.

Where am I? Do the visuals, font and layout tell me the purpose of this site? Is this a high quality site that's been developed by people who are good at what they do? Are the colors, style and formatting appealing to me? Does this site look like other sites I trust?

For the average customer, their assessment is a subconscious one.

And it's fairly simple. They compare your site to something else they've seen. A site they trust or feel good about. It could be their experience as a whole or minor details like availability. Or the fact that your website is pretty. Then they use those factors as a measuring stick to see how you compare.

That assessment is based (almost entirely) on presentation.

When we go to the grocery store presentation is a large part of how we decide. It's not like we can bite into each piece of fruit to see which one tastes the best, so we choose primarily based on looks. It's the same with websites. Most of us have developed an intuition about the personality behind websites. Which is exactly why presentation matters so much.

But presentation is more than just your appearance.

It consists of both tangible and intangible factors that communicate important things about your business to potential customers. These things affect customers and how they respond to you, whether you use them proactively or not. Let's find out how.

Tangible Factors

1. Typography
2. Layout
3. Visuals
4. Color
5. Quality
6. Trust (tangible)

1. Typography

Typography is defined as "the art and technique of arranging type in order to make language visible".[4]

It's an important but commonly overlooked factor in presentation. The reason? Most of us find it boring. So the vast majority of us tend to focus on how a font looks, instead of how well it works.

Immediately this creates problems because the average customer doesn't care about how nice your font looks, they care about clarity and legibility. They want to be able to understand and absorb what they're reading.[5]

Some common mistakes include:

● All caps (body text)

● All caps (headlines)[6]

● All bold

● Right justified

● Fonts that make reading comprehension difficult

● Font manipulation (e.g. weird shapes or "word art")

● Fonts that are smushed together or stretched apart

● Multiple font colors

It's tough to get customers to buy when it's a struggle for them to read and understand what you're saying. People stop reading when typography gets in the way. Which is clearly a problem when you're trying to get them to do something (like give you money).

2. Layout

Poor site layout is common. As a result, customers become confused and disoriented on their web pages. They're unsure about where they are or what they should do next. Leaving is the easiest way to ease their stress and confusion. Not a great spot to be in if you're trying to get them to buy something.

When you choose the right layout it's easy to direct a customer's eyes to where you want them to go. So, what makes a layout great?

Gravity.

Edmund Arnold created the Gutenberg diagram for typography to illustrate the concept of reading gravity.

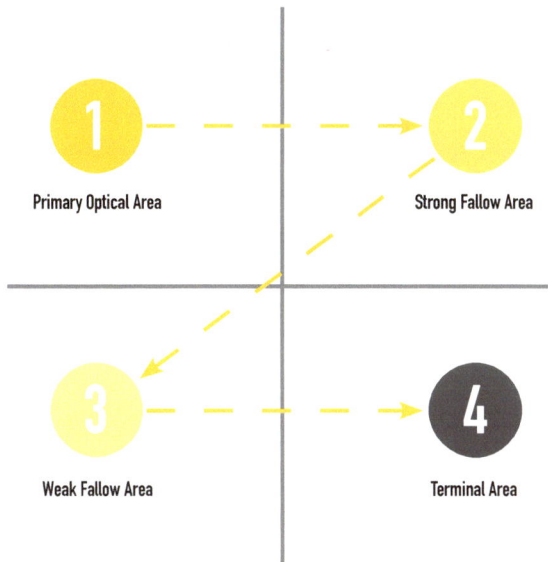

When we learn to read as kids we're taught to start at the top left of the page (primary optical area), going from left to right, back and forth until we reach the bottom right corner (terminal area).

Bad layouts fight against the training we've received. They create confusion, frustration and mental hang-ups in people. That makes it really hard for them to focus on the things you're trying to say, because they're not sure where they should look. Great sales copy won't work if people can't follow what you're saying with their eyes.

3. Visuals

Visuals are neglected. Abused even. We treat them as accessories to words - as if the words themselves were more important than the message. And that's problematic for us because we need pictures. Pictures make the words matter. They give our words meaning.

So we treat visuals like these:

Source: http://www.flickr.com/photos/candiedwomanire/3397197237/

When they're actually this:

Source: http://www.flickr.com/photos/bike/4279344419/

Dan Roam, author of the book, *Blah Blah Blah: What to do when words don't work*, made a pretty profound observation:

> "Pictures aren't training wheels; pictures are the front wheel. When it comes to thinking, talking, and solving problems, it's as if we're all riding around on mental unicycles. Sure, with enough training anyone can learn to ride one, but why bother: We'll always be faster and more stable with two wheels than one." [7]

Which is exactly why stock photography is so harmful when it's abused. Poor visuals take away meaning and they create confusion.

Customers waste time trying to figure out how the generic hand huddle relates to your about section or return policy. See how confusing that is?

Source: http://www.flickr.com/photos/27590831@N06/6836440763/

4. Color

Dr. Alexander Schauss, Ph.D., of the American Institute for Biosocial Research found that "Drunk tank pink" suppressed violent or antagonistic behavior of prisoners:

Calms things down whether you like it or not.

❝

"Even if a person tries to be angry or aggressive in the presence of pink, he can't. The heart muscles can't race fast enough. It's a tranquilizing color that saps your energy. Even the color-blind are tranquilized by pink rooms." [8]

We're drawn to color. Color can increase or decrease our appetite, change our stress levels, and decreases our perception.[9] When we choose the wrong colors, it often creates confusion and a strong reaction.

Color is important, but we don't experience it the same way. Our gender, culture, beliefs, religion and context all shape how we respond to color. It's these differences, these preferences that can be the difference between success or failure.

What if you saw purple, brown, and blue in your stoplight instead of the red, yellow and green you're used to? How would a green stop sign affect drivers? The effects of poor color choices aren't as drastic with your website. No one will die if you choose the wrong color. But spending money with you? That's another story.

5. Quality

Quality is a filter. It sorts and separates likeminded people. Most of us have this habit of believing that beauty + price + demand = quality. But we apply this rule inconsistently.

Some people hold the mistaken belief that beautiful women can't also be intelligent. Then there are those that decide to spend lot of money on incredibly expensive, one off products, like this:

50 thousand dollars for a crocodile skin umbrella

Source: http://www.billionairecouture.com/

The quality of your product should be reflected in the quality of experience. If you're a premium or luxury brand your design needs to look the part. Your pricing needs to look the part. Supply and demand needs to look the part. Your site needs to present a synonymous experience, as if you've given customers a taste of your product.

6. Trust (tangible)

Trust becomes tangible when it's borrowed. When you sell your products on Amazon you have to abide by their rules. Customers know that so it's easier for them to extend their trust in Amazon to you. They know if anything happens, Amazon's got their back.

Something wonderful happens when borrowed trust is nurtured. It becomes your trust. A consistent positive experience means the borrowed trust you started with is now your own.

Intangible Factors

1. Consistency
2. Behavior
3. Ethos
4. Trust (intangible)

1. Consistency

Let's say you're in the grocery store looking for milk. You head to the refridgerated section and pick-up a gallon of milk? What's the first thing you look for on carton? The expiration date. Good for 10 days.

What if the milk's yellow or chunky? What if there's a leak or no expiration date?

What do you do?

You put it back and you look for another carton.

An inconsistent website is like that yellow carton of milk. It says the right things but the message isn't consistent overall. So we put it back. Consistency supports the other presentation factors, but shouldn't be mistaken for something else.

2. Behavior

It's never a good idea to insult customers, which is exactly what Paul Christoforo did. His one man PR shop Ocean Marketing, represented N-Control, makers of the Avenger controller accessory. N-Control accepted preorders for their gaming controller but they failed to deliver on time. Naturally customers were upset.[10]

Paul Christoforo thought slinging insults at customers (and a few other well connected people) was a smart way to put everyone in their place. The internet disagreed, and punished his client N-Control. After the story of Christoforo's behavior went viral, angry gamers took to Amazon posting negative reviews as punishment for his mistake.

N-Control's marketing manager and Christoforo's in-house replacement spent his first week dealing with the fallout.

> *"At this point I'm just trying to point out that, what was said was someone who we hired, what he said should not reflect on the product itself," he said. "So far the Amazon rating on the Avenger has gone from 4 and 1/2 to 1 star in around 8 hours. None of the reviews are true, they all just appeared today out of pure hate trolling."* [11]

Your behavior needs to match your presentation. Luxury brands shouldn't discount their prices, guaranteed overnight delivery shouldn't be two days late and customer centric businesses shouldn't insult their customers.

3. Ethos

Merriam Webster defines Ethos as:[12]

> *The distinguishing character, sentiment, moral nature, or guiding beliefs of a person, group, or institution.*

Sharing your beliefs and what you stand for on your website attracts people similar to you. Those with similar beliefs identify with your business. They can relate to you in a way that's meaningful because you both speak the same language.

Standing for **this**, excludes *that*. If openness is part of your ethos, you're more likely to repel those that value privacy and secrecy above openness. Hiding your ethos attracts people that may not share the same views. That's not necessarily a bad thing however it becomes a problem when it creates conflict and relationship issues.

4. Trust (intangible)

Are you helpful when you respond to email requests? Is your site available when customers need it? Do you deliver on time?

If trust were fire, experience would be the fuel. It's difficult to trust without some kind of experience. We need to take a leap of faith in order for trust to develop. But experience is how it grows.

Trust   **Experience**

When customers buy from you for the first time it's a leap of faith. That leap of faith needs to be based on evidence. Every rewarding experience a customer has with you improves their trust in you.

Every email that's ignored, every order that's unfulfilled, every problem that's glossed over, hurts a customer's trust in you. There will always be problems and mistakes, we're human after all. But you knew that already. What you may not know is the fact that you have control over *how much* it hurts.

Imagine you're doing some online shopping. You've spent a lot of time on research and you know what you want. You're ready to buy. You whip out your credit card and proceed to checkout. You click the payment button and then you see this:

Something went wrong and your customer sees this.

Imagine what it's like to be a customer on the receiving end of this. Did my order go through? Should I go back and try again? Will my card be charged twice? Can someone help me? Do they have live chat? No, maybe if I...

What if your customer saw something different?

What if you gave them a number to call or access to someone they could speak with, anytime? Sure, they're probably frustrated by the fact that something went wrong. But showing them you care, that you'll take care of things for them helps to minimize the damage, and actually increases their trust in you.

Your business is filled with what I call "trust zones", places or areas where problems are likely to occur. Putting the right system in place ahead of time means you're ready to stop the damage when it happens. It also means you're more likely to increase customer trust as a result of your attentiveness and care.

Presentation, as we've seen, is more than just the "look and feel" of your website. These tangible and intangible factors work together, leading your customer to where you want them to go. When there's conflicts or contradictions it creates friction, which makes it harder for customers to do what you want.

Is there a time when presentation doesn't matter?

If you're communicating, it matters. The medium (websites) and individual requirements (design) may change how you present but it doesn't change the rules.

Let's look at three examples.

The job interview: The ultimate goal in a job interview is to get hired. You need to convince your interviewer you're the best candidate for the job. So how do the best candidates present themselves? They dress well, they arrive on time, they focus on the problems their future employer faces, showing how they're the solution, etc. If any one of the things on the list is seriously out-of-whack our resume gets the chop.

Your doctor: What do you expect when you go to your doctor? You expect him to look the part, after all it'd be pretty unprofessional for him to show up in Hawaiian shorts and a Corona beer t-shirt. He has to have good bedside manner.[13] He needs to know his stuff and he needs to know how to prescribe the right medication.

The Police: The law states that we're supposed to obey the police. If an officer tells us to do something we're supposed to listen. But what if we couldn't identify a police officer? Presentation steps in, providing the certainty and protection we need.

Their squad car, uniform and gun give us the visuals we need to authenticate their identity. Their commands and their behavior give us the intangible clarity we need.

Which goes to show that we all rely on presentation.

If you're communicating, you're using it. Those that use it proactively win, because without presentation, there's no fascination, no way to communicate the problem and no way to sell the solution. Presentation is the bedrock of communication.

Those that use it passively end up like Nick. He could have worn a business casual outfit, put his hair in a ponytail or changed his appearance. He didn't look like the professional person that Alex was expecting to meet, which led to an awkward and embarrassing situation. No need to repeat his mistake if we don't have to.

Summary
Why Presentation matters

- We tend to feel bad when we judge someone based on their appearance, but it's part of how we recognize patterns and make sense of the world.

- Judging based on appearance works (with some important exceptions).

- Our appearance is basically a canvas that we paint our personality, values, tastes and temperament on.

- Presentation is more than just appearance. It's a combination of tangible and intangible factors.

- The medium (website, speech, job interview) and requirements (great design) may change with the medium, but the rules remain the same.

- Passive presentation is dangerous; it's likely to create stress and confusion for your customer.

- If you're communicating, your presentation is critical. Most of us do it passively. Those that do it intentionally and proactively will win.

You've finished the book, now what?

If you're like most people, this is a lot to take in. Each component is an important part of getting people to trust in your business. What if you apply things incorrectly? What if you miss something? And how are you supposed to remember everything?

If you need your site to make money, you're going to need help.

No need to worry though, you won't have to do it alone.

We've created HooktoWin.com where you'll get exclusive access to our website wizard and marketing tools. You'll also receive helpful checklists, templates and tools, as well as step-by-step instruction on each of the sections we've covered in this book. Need hand holding or one-on-one support? You can get that too.

Now that you have this information, let us show you how to apply it. Join us at HooktoWin.com. See you there!

Notes

Introduction

1. We've learned from our clients and their businesses. We've also learned from others like Perry Marshall, Dan Roam, Sean D'Souza, Sally Hogshead, Seth Godin, Michael Stelzner, D Bnon Tenant, Jane Straus, Josh Kaufman, Martin Lindstrom, Tom Asacker, Dave Lakhani, W. Chan Kim and Renee Mauborgne, Claude Hopkins, Robert Bly, Beverly Flaxington, Ramit Sethi, Teresa Amabile, Steven Kramer, Jim Collins, and a small army of clients, scientists, gurus, trainers, authors and coaches.

Target Audience: Why the customer you choose controls the amount you'll make

1. "Interview with Manpacks | How to Write a Business Plan." How to Write a Business Plan. N.p., n.d. Web. 13 May 2013. <http://howtowriteabusinessplan.com/2013/03/interview-with-co-founder-of-manpacks-ken-johnson-on-starting-up/>.

2. "Zappos Sends You Flowers – Consumerist." Consumerist. N.p., n.d. Web. 13 Aug. 2013. <http://consumerist.com/2007/10/16/zappos-sends-you-flowers/>.

3. D'Souza, Sean. The brain audit: why customers buy (and why they don't). Auckland, N.Z.: Psychotactics, 2009. Print.

Triggers: You'll never get their attention if you can't fascinate them

1. Hogshead, Sally. Fascinate: your 7 triggers to persuasion and captivation. New York: HarperBusiness, 2010. Print.

2. "Antepenultimate | Define Antepenultimate at Dictionary.com." *Dictionary. com - Free Online English Dictionary.* N.p., n.d. Web. 13 May 2013. <http://dictionary.reference.com/browse/antepenultimate>.

3. Lee, Robyn. "Heart Attack Grill Is Up Front About Slowly Killing You | A Hamburger Today." A Hamburger Today - America's Favorite Hamburger Weblog!. N.p., n.d. Web. 14 Aug. 2013. <http://aht.seriouseats.com/archives/2008/09/heart-attack-grill-burgers-cheeseburgers-chandler-arizona.html>.

4. Miller, Jared T.. "The iPod Turns 10: How It Shaped Music History | TIME.com." Tech | News and reviews from the world of gadgets, gear, apps and the web | TIME.com. N.p., n.d. Web. 13 May 2013. <http://techland.time.com/2011/10/21/the-ipod-turns-10-how-it-shaped-music-history/>.

5. Constine, Josh. "Kids Love The Apple Store So Much They Pee On The Seats | TechCrunch." TechCrunch. N.p., n.d. Web. 14 Aug. 2013. <http://techcrunch.com/2013/03/06/kids-love-apple-too-much/>.

6. Neville, Simon. "iPad 2 fights break out in Apple store lines between customers and scalpers | Mail Online." Home | Mail Online. N.p., n.d. Web. 14 Aug. 2013. <http://www.dailymail.co.uk/sciencetech/article-1367959/iPad-2-fights-break-Apple-store-lines-customers-scalpers.html>.

7. "Is Samsung Copying Apple's Earphones? It sure looks like it - Patently Apple." Patently Apple. N.p., n.d. Web. 13 May 2013. <http://www.patentlyapple.com/patently-apple/2012/09/is-samsung-copying-apples-earphones-it-sure-looks-like-it.html>.

8. "Anthony Weiner sexting scandals - Wikipedia, the free encyclopedia." Wikipedia, the free encyclopedia. N.p., n.d. Web. 14 Aug. 2013. <http://en.wikipedia.org/wiki/Anthony_Weiner_sexting_scandal>.

9. Parker, Ashley. "Hashtags, a New Way for Tweets - Cultural Studies - NYTimes.com." The New York Times - Breaking News, World News & Multimedia. N.p., n.d. Web. 14 Aug. 2013. <http://www.nytimes.com/2011/06/12/fashion/hashtags-a-new-way-for-tweets-cultural-studies.html?pagewanted=all&_r=1&>.

10. "New Car Replacement | Liberty Mutual." Auto Insurance Quotes, Car Insurance Quotes, and Home Insurance | Liberty Mutual. N.p., n.d. Web. 14 Aug. 2013. <http://www.libertymutual.com/auto-insurance/auto-insurance-coverage/auto-insurance-benefits/new-car-replacement>.

11. "Heart Attack Grill, Where a Burger is 8,000 Calories and the Fries are Cooked in Lard." Gourmet Recipes and Restaurant Reviews Blog. N.p., n.d. Web. 14 Aug. 2013. <http://blog.friendseat.com/heart-attack-grill-8000-calorie-burger-and-the-fries-are-cooked-in-lard/>.

Problems: Why we need them, why we're drawn to them

1. Estroff Marano, Hara . "Our Brain's Negative Bias | Psychology Today." Psychology Today: Health, Help, Happiness + Find a Therapist. N.p., n.d. Web. 14 May 2013. <http://www.psychologytoday.com/articles/200306/our-brains-negative-bias>.

2. Kiley Hamlin, J., Karen Wynn, and Paul Bloom. "Three-month-olds Show A Negativity Bias In Their Social Evaluations." Developmental Science 13.6 (2010): 923-929. Print.

3. Hanson, Rick. "Confronting the Negativity Bias: How Your Brain Makes You Easily Intimidated - Rick Hanson | Dr. Rick Hanson - Author of Buddha's Brain and Just One Thing." Dr. Rick Hanson | Author of Buddha's Brain: The Practical Neuroscience of Happiness, Love and Wisdom. N.p., n.d. Web. 14 Aug. 2013. <http://www.rickhanson.net/your-wise-brain/how-your-brain-makes-you-easily-intimidated>.

4. Bosman, Manie. "You Might Not Like it, But Bad is Stronger than Good :: Strategic Leadership Institute." Strategic Leadership Institute. N.p., n.d. Web. 14 Aug. 2013. <http://www.strategicleadershipinstitute.net/news/you-might-not-like-it-but-bad-is-stronger-than-good/>.

5. Tugend, Alina. "Why People Remember Negative Events More Than Positive Ones - NYTimes.com." The New York Times - Breaking News, World News & Multimedia. N.p., n.d. Web. 14 May 2013. <http://www.nytimes.com/2012/03/24/your-money/why-people-remember-negative-events-more-than-positive-ones.html?pagewanted=all&_r=1&>. It's easier for us to remember problems when we're obsessed with them.

6. Perenson, Melissa J.. "Amazon Kindle 2 Vs. Kindle Original: We Compare | PCWorld." PCWorld - News, tips and reviews from the experts on PCs, Windows, and more. N.p., n.d. Web. 14 May 2013. <http://www.pcworld.com/article/160165/amazon_kindle_2.html>.

7. Altucher, James. "Claudia Is Worried I Will Be Killed For Posting... - The Altucher Confidential - Quora." The Altucher Confidential - Quora. N.p., n.d. Web. 12 Aug. 2013. <http://jamesaltucher.quora.com/Claudia-Is-Worried-I-Will-Be-Killed-For-Posting-This>.

Solutions: Why no one cares when you offer yours

1. Leo, Peter. "Cleveland gets testy over bottled water - Pittsburgh Post-Gazette." Pittsburgh Post-Gazette. N.p., n.d. Web. 14 May 2013. <http://www.post-gazette.com/stories/local/morning-file/cleveland-gets-testy-over-bottled-water-442828/>.

2. Gilbert, Sarah. "Fiji Water: So cool, so fresh, so bad for the environment? - DailyFinance." DailyFinance - News and Advice for a Lifetime of Financial Decisions. N.p., n.d. Web. 14 May 2013. <http://www.dailyfinance.com/2009/08/24/tale-of-fiji-water-too-familiar-sounds-like-industrial-colonial/>.

3. Water Technology. "Fiji pulls Cleveland ad campaign." *Water Technology Online - A leading resource for water treatment professionals.* N.p., n.d. Web. 14 May 2013. <http://www.watertechonline.com/articles/fiji-pulls-cleveland-ad-campaign>.

4. "City of Chicago :: Water Treatment." City of Chicago. N.p., n.d. Web. 14 Aug. 2013. <http://www.cityofchicago.org/city/en/depts/water/supp_info/education/water_treatment.html>.

Objections: The inevitable part of selling that gets worse if you run

1. Barnouw, Erik. *Tube of Plenty The Evolution of American Television.* 2nd ed. New York: Oxford University Press, USA, 1990. Print.

Testimonials: Why customers distrust them, how to make yours trustworthy

1. "Case Studies." *WordPress Hosting by Synthesis.* N.p., n.d. Web. 14 May 2013. <http://websynthesis.com/clients/>.

2. "Amazon.com: Cricket "Living life and loving it!"'s review of iRobot Roomba 770 Vacuum Cleaning Robot fo...." *Amazon.com: Online Shopping for Electronics, Apparel, Computers, Books, DVDs & more.* N.p., n.d. Web. 14 May 2013. <http://www.amazon.com/review/R2DFXD89QIRDI8/ref=cm_cr_dp_title?ie=UTF8&ASIN=B005GK3IVW&nodeID=1055398&store=home-garden>.

3. "Client testimonials | David Airey, graphic designer." *David Airey, graphic designer.* N.p., n.d. Web. 14 May 2013. <http://www.davidairey.com/testimonials/>.

4. "How to Get Powerful Testimonials that Convince Even Skeptical Prospects." *Small Business Marketing, Design and Branding Tips.* N.p., n.d. Web. 14 May

2013. <http://www.bigbrandsystem.com/get-testimonials/>.

5. "Six Questions to Ask for Powerful Testimonials | Copyblogger." *Content Marketing Tools and Training | Copyblogger.* N.p., n.d. Web. 14 May 2013. <http://www.copyblogger.com/testimonials-part-2/>.

6. "The Secret Life of Testimonials | Copyblogger." *Content Marketing Tools and Training | Copyblogger.* N.p., n.d. Web. 14 May 2013. <http://www. copyblogger.com/testimonials-part-1/>.

Risk Reversals: Why we struggle to seal the deal

1. Kaufman, Josh. "Risk Reversal." *Personal MBA Book - Josh Kaufman.* N.p., n.d. Web. 14 May 2013. <http://book.personalmba.com/risk-reversal/>.

2. D'Souza, Sean. The brain audit: why customers buy (and why they don't). Auckland, N.Z.: Psychotactics, 2009. Print.

3. ABC15 Arizona. "Valley family pushes to solve new car problems and get GM's attention." *ABC15 Arizona | KNXV-TV Phoenix | News, Weather, Sports, Things To Do.* N.p., n.d. Web. 14 May 2013. <http://www.abc15.com/dpp/money/ consumer/alerts/valley-family-pushes-to-solve-new-car-problems-and-get-general-motors-attention>.

4. "OnStar Privacy Statement - OnStar." *OnStar.* N.p., n.d. Web. 14 May 2013. <https://www.onstar.com/web/portal/privacy?g=1>.

5. Higgins, Tim. "GM Offers Chevy No-Haggle Prices, Money-Back Guarantees - Businessweek." *Businessweek - Business News, Stock market & Financial Advice.* N.p., n.d. Web. 14 May 2013. <http://www.businessweek.com/news/2012-07-10/gm-offers-chevy-no-haggle-prices-money-back-guarantees>.

6. "Used Car Guarantee | 3 Day 150 Mile Guarantee | Certified Pre-Owned ." *Used Chevy|Used Buick|Used GMC | Used Vehicles| Certified Pre-Owned .* N.p., n.d. Web. 14 May 2013. <http://www.gmcertified.com/3-day-150-mile-guarantee>.

7. Collins, Nick. "Ikea recalls cakes in 23 countries after sewage bacteria found - Telegraph." *Telegraph.co.uk - Telegraph online, Daily Telegraph, Sunday Telegraph - Telegraph.* N.p., n.d. Web. 14 May 2013. <http://www.telegraph. co.uk/foodanddrink/foodanddrinknews/9910417/Ikea-recalls-cakes-in-23-countries-after-sewage-bacteria-found.html>.

8. Young, Kimball. "Personality and Early Social Conditioning.." *Social psychology, an analysis of social behavior,.* New York: A.A. Knopf, 1930. 233-270. Print.

9. "Shipping and Returns | Zappos.com." *Shoes, Clothing, and More | Zappos.*

com . N.p., n.d. Web. 14 May 2013. <http://www.zappos.com/shipping-and-returns>.

10. Weisenthal, Joseph. "Zappos Sells More By Encouraging Returns | Techdirt." *Techdirt.* N.p., n.d. Web. 14 May 2013. <http://www.techdirt.com/articles/20070716/093618.shtml>.

Uniqueness: Convincing customers you're the only one for them

1. Putnam, Joseph. "What a Unique Selling Proposition Really Means and Why Your Business MUST Have One." *The @KISSmetrics Marketing Blog.* N.p., n.d. Web. 14 May 2013. <http://blog.kissmetrics.com/unique-selling-proposition/>.

2. "Frederick W. Smith Biography -- Academy of Achievement." *Academy of Achievement Main Menu.* N.p., n.d. Web. 14 May 2013. <http://www.achievement.org/autodoc/page/smi0bio-1>.

3. "Ten things we know to be true - Company - Google ." *Google.* N.p., n.d. Web. 14 May 2013. <http://www.google.com/about/company/philosophy/>.

4. "List of Google products - Wikipedia, the free encyclopedia." *Wikipedia, the free encyclopedia.* N.p., n.d. Web. 14 May 2013. <http://en.wikipedia.org/wiki/List_of_Google_products>.

5. "Top 100 Web Sites (AltaVista) -- PC Magazine." *Internet Archive: Wayback Machine.* N.p., n.d. Web. 14 May 2013. <http://web.archive.org/web/19991005055735/http://www3.zdnet.com/pcmag/special/web100/search1.html>.

6. "Top 100 Web Sites (Google!) -- PC Magazine." *Internet Archive: Wayback Machine.* N.p., n.d. Web. 14 May 2013. <http://web.archive.org/web/19991001132301/http://www8.zdnet.com/pcmag/special/web100/search2.html>.

7. "74212578 - United States Patent and Trademark Office." *United States Patent and Trademark Office.* N.p., n.d. Web. 14 May 2013. <www.uspto.gov/web/offices/com/sol/foia/ttab/other/1998/74212578.pdf>. "Drive Safely" is really that specific. Yet Volvo most of us remember that campaign. How'd they become unique for such a generic phrase? Turns out they bought their uniqueness. In a document filed with the USPTO Volvo asserts that they spent more than $184 million on producing, airing and broadcasting ads for their "Drive Safely" campaign. The USPTO didn't think "Drive Safely" was unique enough and Volvo was forced to appeal.

Presentation: How ignoring it creates confusion, keeps customers from buying

1. Mlodinow, Leonard. "How We Are Judged by Our Appearance | Psychology Today." *Psychology Today: Health, Help, Happiness + Find a Therapist.* N.p., n.d. Web. 14 May 2013. <http://www.psychologytoday.com/blog/subliminal/201206/how-we-are-judged-our-appearance>.

2. Mlodinow, Leonard. "How We Are Judged by Our Appearance | Psychology Today." *Psychology Today: Health, Help, Happiness + Find a Therapist.* N.p., n.d. Web. 14 May 2013. <http://www.psychologytoday.com/blog/subliminal/201206/how-we-are-judged-our-appearance>.

3. "Personality Judgments Based on Physical Appearance." *Personality and Social Psychology* 35.12 (2009): 897-902. SAGE Journals. Web. 14 May 2013.

4. "Typography - Wikipedia, the free encyclopedia." *Wikipedia, the free encyclopedia.* N.p., n.d. Web. 14 May 2013. <http://en.wikipedia.org/wiki/Typography>.

5. Wheildon, Colin, and Geoffrey Heard. *Type & layout: are you communicating or just making pretty shapes.* Rev. ed. Hastings, Vic., Australia: Worsley Press ;, 2005. Print.

6. Does the fact that we used all caps in our cover design make us hypocrites? Not yet. We want to see how this works with everything else (high contrast design, layout, and image) before making a change.

7. Roam, Dan. "Pictures make the words matter - and vice versa." *Blah blah blah: what to do when words don't work.* New York: Portfolio/Penguin, 2011. Kindle Location 589 - 595. Print.

8. Walker, Morton. *The power of color.* Garden City Park, N.Y.: Avery Pub. Group, 1991. Print.

9. "Color & Appetite Matters." *Color Matters welcomes you to the world of color: Symbolism, design, vision, science, marketing and more!.* N.p., n.d. Web. 14 May 2013. <http://www.colormatters.com/color-and-the-body/color-and-appetite-matters>.

10. Krahulik, Mike. "Penny Arcade - Just Wow!." *Penny Arcade - Disney Infinity.* N.p., n.d. Web. 14 May 2013. <http://penny-arcade.com/2011/12/27/just-wow1>.

11. Crecente, Brian. "PR Trolling "Ocean Stratagy" Out of Business, Avenger Controller Maker Asks For Forgiveness." *Kotaku.* N.p., n.d. Web. 14 May 2013. <kotaku.com/5871479/pr-trolling-ocean-stratagy-out-of-business-avenger-controller-maker-asks-for-forgiveness>.

12. "Ethos - Definition and More from the Free Merriam-Webster Dictionary." *Dictionary and Thesaurus - Merriam-Webster Online.* N.p., n.d. Web. 14 May 2013. <http://www.merriam-webster.com/dictionary/ethos>.

13. Blue, Laura. "Better Bedside Manners - TIME." *Breaking News, Analysis, Politics, Blogs, News Photos, Video, Tech Reviews - TIME.com.* N.p., n.d. Web. 14 May 2013. <http://www.time.com/time/health/article/0,8599,1659065,00.html>.

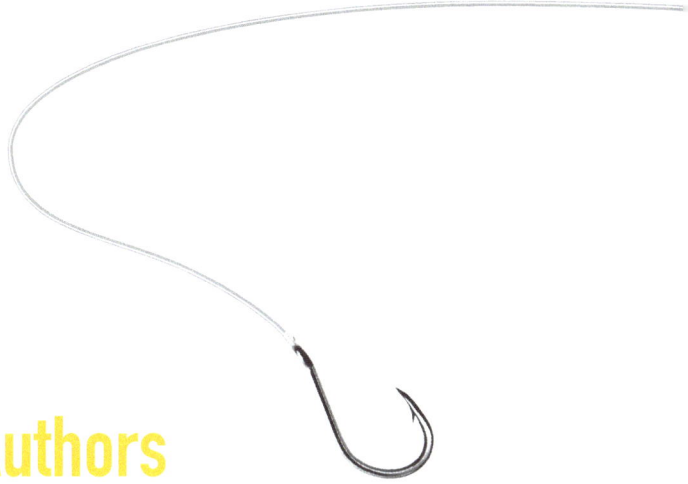

About the Authors

Andrew McDermott is the Co-founder and Marketing Director at WiseToWeb. He has extensive experience building brands, developing strategy and attracting customers. He's worked closely with CEOs, executives and startups as well as mom and pop organizations. He believes what you say is important, but how you say it – that's what sticks.

Rachel McDermott is the Managing Director at WiseToWeb, a development and marketing company located in Milwaukee Wisconsin. She has a Bachelor's Degree in Communication Sciences and Disorders. She believes every interaction that takes place between people depends on the ability to communicate effectively.

Most businesses communicate accidentally. The message they send isn't always the one customers hear. She shows businesses how to communicate so customers will listen.

Andrew and Rachel live with their two sons in Sheboygan, Wisconsin.

About the Publisher

wisetoweb

4230 N. Oakland ave. #159
Shorewood, WI 53211
www.wisetoweb.com

www.ingramcontent.com/pod-product-compliance
Lightning Source LLC
Chambersburg PA
CBHW041313210326
41599CB00008B/259